The Quilted Cottage

Pearl Louise Krush

Published by

 **krause publications**
An F&W Publications Company

700 East State Street • Iola, WI 54990-0001
715-445-2214 • 888-457-2873
www.krause.com

Please call or write for our free catalog of publications. To place
an order or obtain a free catalog, please call 800-258-0929.

Library of Congress Catalog Number: 2003108202
ISBN: 0-87349-700-7

Edited by Nicole Gould
Designed by Sharon Laufenberg

Printed in The United States of America

Acknowledgments

The process of creating a project such as this takes time, cooperation, dedication, and huge amounts of creativity. I would like to thank the following people from my past and my present for all of their influence, love, patience, expertise, and encouragement.

My husband, Fred, for all of his support and encouragement.

My great-grandfather, my grandmothers, and my parents. Their loving influence provided the wonderful childhood memories from which comes all of what I love to do.

My sisters and brother for all the fun-loving memories.

My acquisitions editor, Julie Stephani, who I have known for so many wonderful years and my editor, Niki Gould, who I have known for only a short time but who is fantastic to work with.

My dedicated staff members who are so helpful when pulling a huge project such as this together.

A special thank-you to my friend and assistant, Julie Weaver, who helps me every day as we work our way through the designing process.

What Makes a Cottage?

A cottage can be any home, anywhere. Although you may think of a cottage as a small dwelling such as those found in Hansel and Gretel, Snow White, or Grandma's cottage in Little Red Riding Hood, the cottage style of decorating is really the warm, cozy, comfy feeling that comes when you surround yourself with charming colors, delightful textures, and nostalgic memorabilia. In fact, a growing trend these days is to make something old, new again. Any home, of any size, can be made into your very own cottage.

Color, texture, and contrast are the very basis on which you want to build the "cottage look." Colors can range from soft to bold, but the mix of large, medium, and small designs as well as florals, plaids, and stripes create a "cottage look."

Determine how you want your home to look and how you want your home to feel. Do you want a relaxed feeling when you step into your family room? Do you want to be energized when you walk into your kitchen? Do you want a comfy feeling when you enter your bedroom? You can decide these things by looking through this book and choosing a mood for each of the rooms in your home.

Walls, in addition to the floor and the ceiling, surround each room in a home. These components become your stage on which all of the other designs become the set and actors.

You will need to decide what color the basic room should be. The floor and ceiling should be considered first as they are the areas upon which all other components are based. Do you have hardwood floors under those carpets? Maybe you will want to consider tearing up the carpets and using those floors. If you don't want to go to that

Local craft stores offer inspiration and accessories for your cottage home.

Plants, family photos, and mementos will help you to achieve that cottage look.

much work or expense, consider layering a throw rug over the carpeting to add another accent on the floor. The ceiling of each room is a space that can determine the feeling of the entire room. Paint or paper the ceiling using a medium to dark color, and the room becomes cozier—although perhaps confining, depending on the size of the room. Consider painting the ceiling of the room a shade darker than the walls for a subtle effect. The walls might be painted with a solid or texture treatment, or you might want to consider a selection of coordinating wallpapers. Try not to overdo the number of wallpaper patterns or paint embellishments placed on the walls and ceiling as they may distract from the final decorative performances of your furniture, quilted items, and accent pieces.

For an entirely different look that still achieves the "cottage feel," you can simply change the designs or colors of the fabrics shown on every project in each room. For instance, the master bedroom in this book has been designed using a romantic rose garden fabric. Imagine changing the fabrics to forest lodge plaids and prints in winter colors of deep green, blue, and brown. The basic design stays the same, but the feeling becomes definitely masculine and more "cabin cottage" than "garden cottage." The front porch designs are made using muted red, white, and blue fabrics, but by exchanging them with soft romantic floral fabrics, the result is an inviting "relaxed summer cottage" porch. Using bright red, crisp white, and royal blue prints and stripes could change the basic look and feeling to a clean "energized summer cottage."

As you look through this book, consider how each room makes you feel. You should now be able to look at the rooms in your home and visualize how each room could have the feeling you desire simply by changing a color theme and fabric choice. Do you need some new furniture to complete the room? Where are some of those old photos or other pieces of memorabilia that you can add to the room for a touch of heritage? New plants always

Old quilts (or new ones!), throw rugs, and greenery add that cozy, comfy feeling.

Add warmth and charm to your home with candles and cherished photographs.

add a touch of life to any room. Shop flea markets, yard sales, auctions, and you will find many small accent pieces to add to your cottage.

You can find inspiration for your cottage rooms throughout this book, in many wonderful magazines, and home based television programs. Make notes about the items that inspire and excite you. Gather together all of the notes, photos, and fabric samples that you love and create a storyboard before you begin.

A storyboard is a basic foam core board on which you will place all of the things you want in each room. This will help when it comes time to choose paint, wallpaper, fabric, furnishings, and accent pieces. It will also help to create a working budget.

Wonderful accent pieces can be found at flea markets, yard sales, and auctions.

Making a Storyboard

Materials and Tools Needed

- 12" x 18" foam core board
- Push pins or glue
- Paint chip samples
- Wall paper samples
- Fabric samples
- Clippings of "ideas"
- Other samples such as trim

Cottage Quilt Basics

Color Choices

Color is the starting point for any decorating project. When shopping for fabrics to make any of the projects included in this book, bring your storyboard with you and look for colors that fill your design concept.

Natural Backgrounds of cream and beige provide a soft foundation upon which all designs can be built.

Medium Mellow Tones of gold, brown, orange, and rose will add warmth and romance to any design.

Dark Rich Colors such as red, green, blue, and brown will offset the other chosen hues.

Fabric Choices

100% cotton fabrics are suggested for all of the Quilted Cottage projects. The choices for fabrics are so wide and varied, it is best to have an idea of what you are looking for before you go shopping. You will need to choose a variety of fabrics to have the best results when making any of the projects. To attain the "cottage look," you will need to look for the following:

Medium and Large Scale Prints

These prints are used sparingly because of their size. They would sometimes be considered the "story" fabrics as they may contain all or most of the colors that are needed to complete your current project. This type of fabric is best used in the largest portion of any block or borders. It should not be cut into too many sections to make a block as the design will be lost. Large cabbage rose prints are an example of this type of fabric.

Plaids, Checks, and Stripes

These prints add a touch of charm to any design. Sometimes it is important that the designs be cut on the grain line to have a very tailored effect. This may be important on borders or large portions on blocks. In most cases, the plaids, checks, and stripes are being cut into small pieces that are then sewn into blocks. The design of each block becomes more important than the straight cut on any of these prints.

Small Prints

Small prints are the basics of cottage design. The small prints can include anything: dots, flowers, stars, paisleys. These darling prints can be used as quiet backgrounds or bold patterns that add a spark to the quilted project. Any small print will work, as long as it contains the color and design that complement the overall concept you are trying to achieve.

Backgrounds and Tone-on-Tone Prints

Cream, beige, and tan prints are used as backgrounds on many of the Quilted Cottage projects. Don't forget other tone-on-tone prints that are now available as viable choices for background fabrics. These fabrics are sometimes referred to as printed solids. The printed tone-on-tone fabrics are wonderful backgrounds and far exceed solid fabrics used for backgrounds because your eye continues to move over the entire design of the project. Solid fabrics tend to make your eyes stop.

Look at other quilts or blocks that contain both print and solid fabrics as backgrounds and you will understand why it is recommended that you choose a printed background for quilts that are being made today.

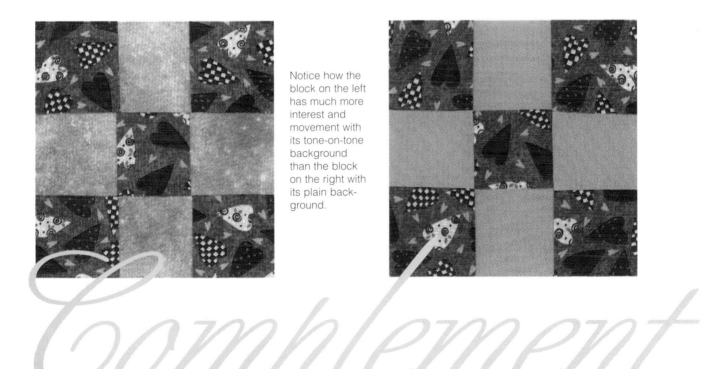

Notice how the block on the left has much more interest and movement with its tone-on-tone background than the block on the right with its plain background.

Backing Fabrics

Choose a printed fabric to provide the backing on any of the projects. You may want to piece the back on the quilts for additional interest. Large, medium, or small scale prints will work for quilt backs as long as they have colors and themes complimentary to those contained on the quilt top. Solid backs are not suggested as they do not do justice to all of the work that has been completed on the quilt top.

Binding Fabrics

The binding on any quilt should be the final frame on the quilt. The binding can be one of the fabrics that is used in any of the blocks, or the same fabric that has been used on the final border.

Basics, Basics, and More Basics

When constructing any of the quilt projects, the following components are important to keep in mind.

Batting

Choose a batting that allows the block and quilt design to shine. The Warm & Natural® thin cotton batting was used on all of *The Quilted Cottage* projects. This batting reminds me of my grandmother's quilts. It is soft and pliable. The fabrics meld with the batting, and it is wonderful for both machine and hand quilting. There are many fantastic battings now available on the market. After you purchase the batting of your choice, remove it from the bag and allow it to rest before you layer and quilt your current project.

Thread

Don't forget thread! Choose a good quality thread that matches the basic colors of the fabrics you are using to build the blocks. Inexpensive thread can become a nightmare when it tangles or frays as you are sewing the quilt blocks together. You will need to make another thread choice to quilt the quilt. For machine quilting, there are many beautiful decorative threads that you might want to consider. Variegated threads would be great when used on many of the projects in *The Quilted Cottage*. Metallic threads, however, would not be a good choice as the metallic threads tend to add a contemporary twist to the design. Choosing a hand quilting thread is another important element if you are hand quilting any of the projects. Choose good quality hand quilting threads that complement the color of the project you are quilting.

Matching threads in a decorative machine stitch are used to secure the appliqué design while a coordinating thread is used for the echo quilting that highlights the design.

And Don't Forget ...

Refer often to your storyboard to make sure you are not straying away from your original plan. Look for fabrics that complement each other. Don't try to "match" every fabric. Remember to allow some variety such as the checks, dots, stripes, or plaids to be a part of the plan. When you allow a few unusual elements to become a part of your quilt, the entire quilt comes to life. Have the sales person lay the fabrics you have chosen together on the counter and step back to have a really good look at your choices before the fabric is cut. Take time to plan and play. You will be amazed at how changing one fabric can bring the quilt project together.

All of the instructions are based on 44" wide fabric. Fabric needed requirements are based on 40" with an additional amount given for cutting errors and stash. Even the most experienced quilter makes cutting errors at times. The fabric may also shrink. It is always best to purchase slightly more fabric than suggested in case you want to make additional accessory projects.

I would suggest that you wash, dry, and press all fabrics before cutting. Hand wash and machine dry smaller cuts of fabrics as they tend to tangle when placed in a washing machine. Larger fabric cuts can be washed in warm water in a washing machine. Machine dry and press the fabrics.

Complementary fabrics, rather than matching ones, offer interest and the comfortable, homemade feeling that we expect in the cottage look.

Hand-appliquéd with a blanket stitch, the stars add a touch of whimsy to this patriotic banner.

General Instructions and Tools

Cutting Supplies and Instructions:

1. Cutting instructions are based on 42" wide 100 percent cotton fabrics.

2. ¼" seams are allowed on all pieced and sewn seams.

3. For accurate cutting, a rotary cutter, cutting mat, and see-through ruler are required.

4. It is best to checkmark each cut as you complete it for accuracy.

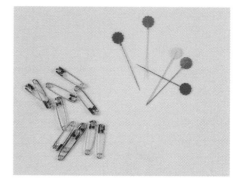

Sewing Supplies and Instructions

The basic sewing supplies that are needed are:

Pins

■ Flower head pins or silk pins are best for pinning seams before sewing.

■ 1" safety pins are best for pinning the layers of fabrics and batting together before quilting.

Scissors

■ Good quality scissors are a must for quilt making. Use the good scissors for fabric cutting only.

■ A pair of regular scissors is needed for paper cutting.

■ A short blade serrated scissors is used for the clipping on the chenille and rag time quilts.

■ A small pair of embroidery scissors is needed for the embroidery and hand work techniques.

Thread

■ Use a quality 100 percent cotton thread or poly-wrapped cotton thread for piecing and sewing the projects together.

■ Use any type of decorative thread or quality quilt thread for quilting.

■ DMC® embroidery floss was used on the stitched projects and quilts in this book. Other embroidery items needed are an 8" embroidery hoop and an embroidery needle.

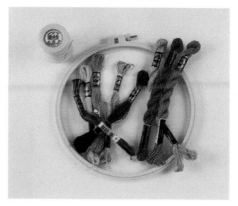

Ironing Board and Iron

- An ironing board that can be placed at different levels is very useful. If at all possible, place the ironing board next to your sewing machine table at the same height as the sewing machine table or cabinet.
- A clean steam iron is needed to press all the seams, the iron-on interfacing, and the iron-on fusible web products.
- Press all seams to the dark fabric when possible. Also press the seams in opposite directions which will allow them to "lock."

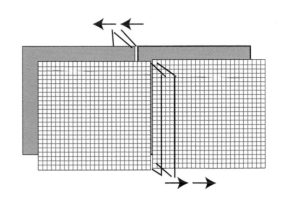

Iron-on Fusible Web

There is a wide assortment of iron-on fusible web products on the market today. The product used on the projects in this book is Steam-a-Seam 2® from the Warm Company. The basic product consists of a web of glue that is placed between two sheets of paper. Read the instructions provided with the product you are using. Trace around the appliqué shapes required onto one of the paper sides on the iron-on fusible web. Peel off the back paper and press the iron-on fusible web to the wrong side of the fabric selected for that appliqué. Cut out the appliqué on the traced lines. Peel off the paper backing. Place the appliqué on the project and press in place. Machine sew around each appliqué using a straight stitch or decorative stitch. Hand embroidery stitches add a dimensional touch to the appliqué design.

Iron-on Interfacing

Iron-on interfacing is a web product that has a fusible side. The iron-on interfacing comes in many weights. The light weight product is recommended for the appliqué scallops on the Bed of Roses Quilt. This product can be sewn on to a shape to add dimension and smooth outer edges on curved shapes. The product can also be sewn on to allow the appliqué shape to be ironed in place before it is attached with decorative stitches. The fusible side can be placed inside the shape, adhering the top and back fabrics before sewing the appliqués in place.

Lining

The lining you use for the valances should be a product that blocks the ultraviolet light, or the front fabrics will fade. The Roclon® Thermalsuede® lining from Rockland Industries, Inc. is available in white and ivory. Most fabric stores that sell home decorating fabrics carry it.

Sewing Machines and Attachments

■ A clean sewing machine in good working condition that sews a straight stitch is all that is required for piecing together a quilt.

■ Should you have a machine that does decorative stitches, choose a favorite decorative stitch to sew around each appliqué. The blanket stitch was used extensively to sew around each of the appliqués on the projects shown.

■ The feed dogs on the machine need to be in the down position or covered with a protective plate to sew the meander, stippling, or free form of quilting. The darning foot is needed as the attachment.

■ The walking foot attachment is another very functional foot that is used to machine quilt with the technique known as stitch in the ditch. The walking foot allows all the layers of fabric to be fed through the sewing machine at equal intervals.

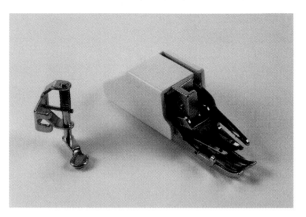

Easy Corner and Triangle Blocks

Throughout this book there will be projects that require corner-square triangles, half-square triangles, and quarter-square triangles. The following diagrams will help with the construction of these blocks.

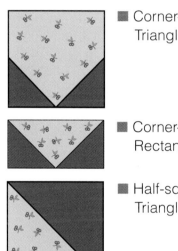

■ Corner-square Triangles

■ Corner-square Rectangles

■ Half-square Triangles

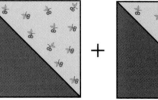

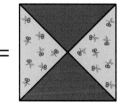

■ Quarter-square Triangles

Strip Piecing

It is easy to make the checkerboard borders that are shown on projects in this book by using this method.

1. Sew two strips of light and dark fabrics together lengthwise. Crosscut these strips into equal units as stated in the pattern instructions.

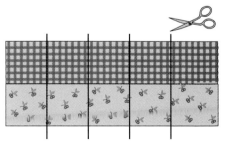

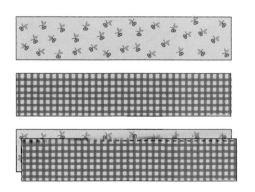

2. Pair the units right sides together with opposite fabrics touching. Sew together.

3. Sew as many of the units together as are required. Open and press to the darker fabric.

4. To make the wide checkerboard border, sew four rows of alternating fabrics together. Make two sets of strip sets. Crosscut into the width required. Press. Sew the units together, locking seams, until the length required is sewn and pressed.

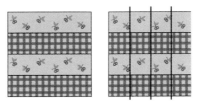

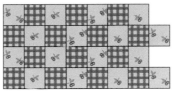

Embroidery Stitches

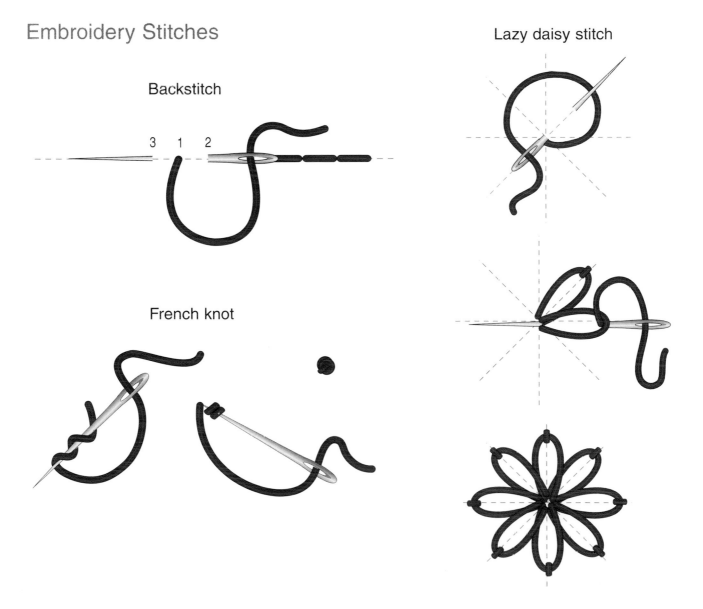

Backstitch

French knot

Lazy daisy stitch

Yo-yos

Several projects in this book call for yo-yos. The small, gathered fabric circles are easy to make.

1. Thread the needle with two strands of thread. Knot the thread ends.

2. Fold the outer edge of each yo-yo to the center on the wrong side about ⅛".

3. Insert the needle and hand sew large (¼") gathering stitches around the entire circle.

4. Pull the thread tight. Tie off and clip the thread ends.

Pillow Backs

There are many methods for finishing a pillow. Here is an easy one.

1. Fold one edge on each pillow back rectangle under ½" to make a hem. Sew in place.

2. With right sides up, overlap the hemmed edges and topstitch 1" on the ends to hold in place.

3. Place the pillow top and back fabrics right sides together. Sew around the entire pillow. Turn right-side out through the opening.

4. Insert the pillow form. Place a small amount of stuffing in the corners to make a tight fit if desired.

5. Hand sew the pillow opening shut.

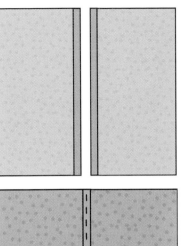

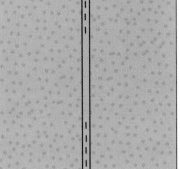

Chapter 1

Americana Cottage Porch

Invite your family and friends to join you on your very own Americana deck or porch. The colors of summer and liberty are combined to piece together the lap quilt, table cover, pillows, and wall quilt.

Display the quilts and pillows on old wicker chairs or new deck furniture ... it won't matter because everyone will feel comfy and welcome.

Barbecues, picnics, or ice cream socials will add more festiveness to this celebration collection.

All of these quilted projects would also look great throughout the rest of your home.

Home

Cool Summer Nights Throw

60" x 60" Throw Quilt

Watch the glimmering stars when you cuddle under this throw quilt on those cool summer nights. The charming large red floral print adds a touch of romantic charm to the celebration colors of red, white, and blue. Notice the chain of cream print and blue prints connecting the blocks from side to side. The large red floral print makes each of the remaining blocks jump forward to catch your eye. This cozy summer porch quilt is very simple to make.

Preparation

1. Read all instructions before you begin.
2. Wash and press all fabrics.
3. Use ¼" seams throughout.
4. Press seam allowances in the direction that allows the seam to "lock" before continuing to build each portion of each block. Press all seams to the dark fabric when possible.
5. Cutting instructions are based on 42" wide fabrics.

Fabric and Tools Needed

- 1⅔ yd. large red floral print for Stone and Mortar blocks and border
- 1 yd. cream print for 16-Patch blocks, Stone and Mortar blocks, and cornerstones
- ⅓ yd. small red print for 16-Patch blocks
- ⅓ yd. tan check for 16-Patch blocks
- 1 yd. small blue print for 16-Patch blocks, Stone and Mortar blocks, cornerstones, and large border cornerstones
- 1⅛ yd. blue and tan print for lattice
- ⅔ yd. small red floral print for binding
- 4 yd. backing fabric
- 64" square thin cotton batting
- Basic sewing supplies, rotary cutter, cutting mat, and see-through ruler

Cutting Instructions

From the large red floral print, cut

- (2) 4½" x 42" strips

  From these strips, cut (12) 4½" squares for the center square on the Stone and Mortar blocks.

- (2) 2⅞" x 42" strips

  From these strips, cut (26) 2⅞" squares for the half-square triangle squares on the Stone and Mortar blocks.

- (8) 4½" x 42" strips for the border

  Sew four sets of two border strips end-to-end.

From the cream print, cut

- (11) 2½" x 42" strips

  From two of these strips, cut (18) 2½" squares for the cornerstones.

  From six of these strips, cut (48) 2½" x 4½" for the rectangles on the Stone and Mortar blocks.

  The four remaining strips are for the 16-Patch blocks.

From the small red print, cut

- (4) 2½" x 42" strips for the 16-Patch blocks

From the tan check, cut

- (4) 2½" x 42" strips for the 16-Patch blocks

From the small blue print, cut

- (6) 2½" x 42" strips

  From two of these strips, cut (18) 2½" squares for the cornerstone squares.

  The remaining four strips are for the 16-Patch blocks.

- (3) 2⅞" x 42" strips

  From these strips, cut (26) 2⅞" squares for the half-square triangle squares on the Stone and Mortar blocks.

- (1) 4½" x 22" strip

  Cut this strip into four 4½" squares for the border cornerstones.

From the blue and tan print, cut

- (15) 2½" x 42" strips

  Cut these strips into (60) 2½" x 8½" rectangles for the lattice.

From the small red floral print, cut

- (6) 2½" x 42" strips for the binding

From the backing fabric, cut

- (2) 2 yd. lengths

Building the Blocks

16-Patch Blocks – Make 13

Sewing four Four-Patch blocks together makes the 16-Patch blocks. Unit A consists of the tan check and small blue print. Unit B consists of the small red print and the cream print.

1. Place a tan check 2½" x 42" strip right sides together on a small blue print 2½" x 42" strip. Sew together on the 42" side. Make four strip sets.

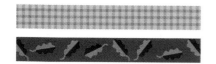 

2. Crosscut the sewn strips into (52) 2½" x 4½" rectangles.

3. Lay the blue print end of the rectangle right sides together on the tan print end of the rectangle, right sides together in pairs. Sew together to make 26 Four-Patch Unit A's.

4. Place a cream print 2½" x 42" strip right sides together on a small red print 2½" x 42" strip. Sew together on the 42" side. Make four strip sets.

Unit A

5. Crosscut the sewn strips into (52) 2½" x 4½" rectangles.

6. Lay the red print end of the rectangle right sides together on the cream print end of the rectangle, right sides together in pairs. Sew together to make 26 Four-Patch Unit B's.

7. Refer to the 16-Patch block diagram and place the tan and blue Unit A's right sides together on the red and cream unit B's. Sew together and press. Referring to the 16-Patch diagram, arrange the top and bottom of each square right sides together. Sew together and press.

Unit B

8. Lay the (13) 16-Patch blocks to the side.

16-Patch Block

Stone and Mortar Blocks – Make 12

The Stone and Mortar blocks are made of half-square triangles, rectangles, and a large center square. Unit A consists of the small blue print and large red floral half-square triangles sewn to the cream print rectangles. Unit B consists of cream print rectangles sewn to the large red floral print center square.

1. Draw a diagonal line across the wrong side of each of the 2⅞" small blue print squares. Place the 2⅞" large red floral print squares right sides together on the small blue print squares. Sew a ¼" seam on each side of the drawn line. Cut apart on the drawn line. Open and press. Square to 2½".

2. Refer to the Stone and Mortar diagram. Sew the large red floral side of 48 half-square triangles to the ends of (24) 2½" x 4½" cream print rectangles. Press.

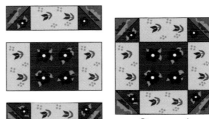

3. Sew the remaining 2½" x 4½" rectangles to the top and bottom of the 4½" large red floral center squares. Press.

4. Lay the 12 blocks to the side.

Stone and
Mortar Block

Lattice

There are six rows of lattice. Each row of lattice consists of five 2½" x 8½" blue and tan print rectangles.

1. Sew a cream print 2½" cornerstone to one end of 18 of the blue and tan 2½" x 8½" rectangles.

2. Sew a small blue print 2½" cornerstone to the remaining end of the 18 rectangles from Step 1.

3. Alternate three lattice pieces with cornerstones and two plain lattice pieces.

4. Sew three rows of lattice together, starting with a cream print cornerstone and ending with a small blue print cornerstone. Sew three rows of lattice, starting with the small blue print cornerstone and ending with a cream print cornerstone.

5. Referring to the photo, assemble the block rows. Sew a 2½" x 8½" lattice rectangle to the left-hand side of each Stone and Mortar block. Sew rows of five blocks together. Sew a 2½" x 8½" lattice rectangle to right-hand side of the last block in each row.

Building the Quilt

1. Refer to the quilt layout photo. Pin a lattice strip to the top of each row of blocks. Carefully align the corner-square seams to match. Sew in place. Sew the remaining lattice strip to the bottom of the last row of blocks.

2. Measure across the quilt to get an exact measurement for the top and bottom border. Add ½" to the measurement. Sew the 4½" small blue print cornerstone square to the ends of the top and bottom border. Press. Measure the sides of the quilt to get the exact measurement. Add a ½" seam allowance. Sew the side borders on the quilt. Sew the top and bottom border in place. Press.

Finishing the Quilt

1. Cut the quilt back into two 2-yard pieces. Sew the 72" sides of the fabrics together. Trim off the excess fabric so that the back measures 68" square.

2. Cut the batting to fit the backing.

3. Layer the batting between the top and back of the quilt. Pin and quilt as desired. Our example was meander stitched over the entire quilt with separate coordinating threads in the red floral areas.

4. Sew the six small red floral binding strips end-to-end. Fold right sides together and press. Starting on the center edge of one side, pin and sew the raw edge of the binding to the quilt. Miter the corners as the binding is sewn on. Turn the folded edge of the binding to the back and hand sew in place.

Peaceful Star Pillow

16" Pillow

This vibrant pillow features beautiful romantic floral prints as well as basic star print fabrics. The quarter-square triangles blended with half-square triangles make the star points shine, even on a bright summer day.

Preparation

1. Read all instructions before you begin.
2. Wash, dry, and press all fabrics.
3. Use ¼" seams throughout.
4. Press seam allowances in the direction that allows the seams to "lock" before continuing to build each block. Press all seams to the dark fabric when possible.
5. Cutting instructions are based on 42" wide fabrics.

Fabric and Tools Needed

- Fat quarter or 18" x 22" of the following fabrics:
  - large red floral print
  - cream and red star print
  - blue star print
- backing fabric
- 16" pillow form or polyester fiberfill stuffing
- Basic sewing supplies, rotary cutter, cutting mat, and see-through ruler

Cutting Instructions

From the large red floral print, cut

- (1) 4½" square.
- (1) 5¼" square
- (4) 2½" squares

From the cream and red star print, cut

- (4) 2½" squares
- (4) 2½ x 4½" rectangles
- (1) 5¼" square

From the blue star print, cut

- (2) 4⅞" squares
- (2) 2½" x 12½" rectangles
- (2) 2½" x 16½" rectangles

From the backing fabric, cut

- (2) 9" x 16½" rectangles

Making the Blocks

1. To make the half-square triangles, draw a diagonal line across the wrong side of the cream and red star print fabric 5¼" square. Place right sides together on the 5¼" large red floral print square. Sew a ¼" seam on each side of the drawn line. Cut apart on the drawn line. Open and press.

2. Draw a diagonal line across the wrong side on the 4⅞" blue star print squares. Place the half-square triangles from step 1 right sides together on the 4⅞" blue star print squares. Sew a ¼" seam on each side of the diagonal line drawn on the blue print squares. Cut apart on the drawn line. Open and press.

3. Square off each of the four squares to 4½". Lay to the side.

Making the Corner-Square Units

1. Place the 2½" large red floral square right sides together with one 2½" cream and red star fabric square. Sew together. Make four of these corner-square units.

2. Refer to the photo and sew a 2½" x 4½" rectangle to the sides of the corner-square units, placing the large red floral square on the outer corner of each unit.

Making the Pillow

1. Lay out each section of the pillow as shown in the pillow diagram. Sew the blue sides of the half-square triangle units to the top and bottom of the center square. Press.

2. Sew a cornerstone unit to each side of a half-square triangle unit to make both the right-hand side and left-hand side of the pillow top. Press.

3. Sew the sides to the pillow center. Press.

4. Sew a 2½" x 12½" blue star print rectangle to the sides of the pillow.

5. Sew a 16½" blue star print rectangle to the top and bottom of the pillow front. Press.

6. Place the cotton batting under the pillow top and quilt as desired. The model shown was meander-stitched over the entire pillow top. (If your sewing machine doesn't work well quilting on the batting, you may need to place an 18" square of muslin on the bottom for stabilizing.) Trim the batting and muslin even with the pillow top.

7. Sew a ½" hem on one of the 16½" edges on the pillow back fabrics. Repeat on the remaining back fabric piece. Overlap the hemmed edges and top stitch on each side to hold in place.

8. Place the backing right sides together on the quilted pillow top. Sew around. Turn right side out through the back opening.

9. Insert the pillow form or stuffing. Hand sew the opening shut. (See page 21 for more information on finishing pillows.)

Small Berry Star Pillow

12" Pillow

This charming cottage pillow features star points made of small cherry print fabric along with small red, blue, and gold prints. The pillow is easily pieced in no time at all.

Preparation

1. Read all instructions before you begin.
2. Wash, dry, and press all fabrics.
3. Use ¼" seams throughout.
4. Press seam allowances in the direction that allows the seams to "lock" before continuing to build each block. Press all seams to the dark fabric when possible.
5. Cutting instructions are based on 42" wide fabrics.

Fabric and Tools Needed

- Fat quarter or 18" x 22" of the following fabrics:
  - small red print
  - small blue print
  - cream and red berry print
- pillow backing fabric
- Fat eighth or 9" x 22" small gold print
- 12" pillow form and polyester fiberfill

Cutting Instructions

From the small red print, cut

- (1) 6¼" square
- (2) 2" x 10½" rectangles
- (2) 2" x 12½" rectangles

From the small gold print, cut

- (1) 6¼" square

From the cream and red print, cut

- (2) 3" x 18" strips

  From these strips, cut eight 3" squares.

From the small blue print, cut

- (2) 3" x 22" strips

  From these strips, cut four 3" x 5½" rectangles and four 3" squares.

From the pillow backing fabric, cut

- (2) 7" x 12½" rectangles

Making the Pillow

1. Draw a diagonal line across the wrong side of the small gold print 6¼" square.

   Place the small gold print square right sides together on the small red print 6¼" square. Sew a ¼" seam on each side of the drawn line. Cut apart on the drawn line. Open and press.

2. Draw a diagonal line across the back of one half-square triangle block. Place the half-square triangles right sides together with opposite fabrics touching.

3. Sew a ¼" seam on each side of the drawn line. Cut apart on the drawn line. Open and press. Square one block to 5½". Only one 5½" quarter-square triangle will be used.

4. Draw a diagonal line on the wrong side of the eight 3" small cream and red print squares.

5. Place a cream and red square right sides together on one end of all of the four small blue print rectangles. Sew on the drawn line. Trim off the back fabrics leaving a ¼" seam. Press.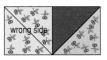

   Repeat this process on the remaining end on each small blue print rectangle.

6. Sew a 3" small blue print square to the end of two of the rectangles to make the side panels.

7. Sew a star point rectangle to each side of the center square to make the center pillow panel. Refer to photo for layout. Press.

8. Sew the side panels to the pillow center panel. Press.

9. Sew a 2" x 10½" small red print border rectangle to the top and bottom of the pillow.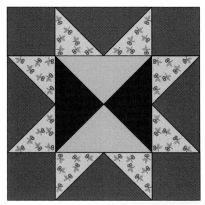

10. Sew a 2" x 12½" small red print border rectangle to the sides of the pillow.

11. Fold one 12½" edge on each pillow back rectangle under ½" to make a hem. Sew in place.

12. With right sides up, overlap the hemmed edges and topstitch 1" on the ends to hold in place.

13. Place the pillow top and back fabrics right sides together. Sew around the entire pillow. Turn right side out through the opening.

14. Insert the pillow form. Place a small amount of stuffing in the corners (if desired) to make a tight fit.

15. Hand sew the pillow opening shut. (See page 21 for more information on finishing pillows.)

Charming

Yo-Yo Flag Pillow

13½" x 10" Pillow

The yo-yo pillow brings back many cherished memories of days gone by. Yo-yos are easily stitched and, when placed together, they make a charming nostalgic statement. This pillow is made with soft red, tan, and blue prints all placed on a romantic background fabric.

Preparation

1. Read all instructions before you begin.
2. Wash, dry, and press all fabrics.
3. Use ¼" seams throughout.
4. Cutting instructions are based on 42" wide fabric.

Fabric and Tools Needed

■ Fat quarter or 18" x 22" of the following fabrics:

  ▶ soft blue print

  ▶ soft red print

  ▶ soft tan print

  ▶ rose print background fabric

■ Polyester fiberfill stuffing
■ Thread to match all fabrics
■ Yo-yo pattern (page 124)
■ Basic sewing supplies

Cutting Instructions

From the soft blue print, cut

■ 12 yo-yos

From the soft red print, cut

■ 32 yo-yos

From the soft tan print, cut

■ 26 yo-yos

From the rose print backing fabric, cut

■ (1) 14" x 22" rectangle

Making the Pillow

1. Thread the needle with two strands of thread. Knot the thread ends. Fold the outer edge of each yo-yo to the center on the wrong side about ⅛". Insert the needle and hand sew large (¼") gathering stitches around the entire circle. Pull the thread tight. Tie off and clip the thread ends. Repeat this process on all of the yo-yos. (See page 20 for more information on making yo-yos.)

2. Refer to the pillow photo. Thread the needle with a single strand of matching thread and tack the blue yo-yos together.

3. Tack the remaining yo-yos together making three rows of six and four rows of 10 yo-yos.

4. Tack each row together to make the flag. Set aside.

5. Fold and sew a ½" hem on each 14" edge of the backing fabric rectangle. Overlap the hemmed ends and top sew each end 1".

6. With right sides together, fold the pillow backing so that the seam is placed at the center. Sew the side seams. Turn right side out through the opening.

7. Stuff the pillow firmly. (See page 21 for more information on finishing pillows.)

8. Hand sew the opening shut. Tack the yo-yo flag to the center front of the pillow to finish.

Twin Star Table Cover

50" x 50" Square Table Cover

Serve your guests a delightful glass of lemonade on this beautiful table quilt. The table quilt is large enough to use on a 42" table or a small 24" garden table. Machine sew the binding on this table cover to make it more durable as it may need to be washed quite often.

Preparation

1. Read all instructions before you begin.
2. Wash, dry, and press all fabrics.
3. Use ¼" seams throughout.
4. Press all seam allowances in the direction that allows them to "lock." Press seams to the dark fabric when possible.
5. Cutting instructions are based on 42" wide fabric.

Fabrics and Tools Needed

- ¾ yd. red print for stars
- 1⅓ yd. small gold/tan print for center panel and wide border
- 1⅓ yd. medium blue print for checkerboard border, outside border, and binding
- ¾ yd. medium blue and cream print for second border and star cornerstone blocks
- ½ yd. white-on-white print for checkerboard border
- 3 yd. backing fabric
- 54" square thin cotton batting
- Thread
- Basic sewing supplies, rotary cutter, cutting mat, and see-through ruler

Cutting Instructions

From the gold/tan print, cut

- (1) 7¼" x 42" strip

    From this strip, cut two 7¼" squares and four 6½" squares.

- (4) 9½" x 30½" rectangles for the wide border

From the red print, cut

- (1) 6½" square for the large star center
- (2) 7¼" squares for the large star points and center quarter-square triangle block
- (4) 3½" squares for the four cornerstone quarter-square triangle centers
- (8) 4¼" squares for the four corner-square triangle blocks

From the medium blue print, cut

- (8) 1½" x 42" strips for the checkerboard pieced border
- (6) 2½" x 42" strips for the outer border
- (6) 2½" x 42" strips for binding

From the medium blue and cream print, cut

- (4) 2½" strips for the second border
- (1) 4¼" x 42" strips

    From this strip, cut eight 4¼" squares for the cornerstone quarter-square triangle blocks.

- (2) 3½" x 42" strips

    From these strips, cut (16) 3½" squares for the cornerstone quarter-square triangle blocks.

From the white-on-white print, cut

- (8) 1½" strips for the checkerboard border

From the backing fabric, cut

- (2) 1½ yd. lengths

From the batting, cut

- (1) 54" x 54" square

Delightful

Making the Blocks

Quarter-Square Triangle Cornerstone Blocks – Make Four

1. Draw a diagonal line across the wrong side of the eight 4¼" red print squares.

2. Place the squares with the drawn lines right sides together on the medium blue and cream 4¼" squares.

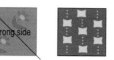

3. Sew a ¼" seam on each side of the drawn line. Cut apart on the drawn line. Open and press.

4. Draw a diagonal line across the back of eight triangle squares. Place two of the squares right sides together with the red print triangle on the blue print triangle. Sew a ¼" seam on each side of the drawn line. Cut on the drawn line. Open and press. Trim the excess fabric "ears."

5. Lay out each block as shown, alternating the quarter-square triangles with the 3½" medium blue and cream squares and the 3½" red print square for the center. Sew each section of three pieces together. Press. Sew the three rows of each block together. Press and lay to the side.

Large Quarter-Square Triangle Block – Make One

1. Draw a diagonal line across the back of the small gold/tan 7¼" squares.

2. Place the squares with the drawn lines right sides together on the red print 7¼" square. Sew a ¼" seam on each side of the drawn line. Cut on the drawn line. Open and press.

3. Draw a diagonal line across the wrong side of two of the half-square triangle blocks. Place the red print portion of the half-square triangle block right sides together on the gold/tan print portion of the half-square triangle block. Sew a ¼" seam on each side of the drawn line. Cut apart on the drawn line. Open and press. Trim off the "ears."

4. Lay out the star block as shown in photo, alternating the quarter-square triangles with the 6½" gold/tan squares and the 6½" red print square for the center. Sew the three portions of each row together. Sew the three rows together. Press and lay to the side.

Pieced Checkerboard Border

1. Sew the white-on-white print 1½" x 42" strips onto the 1½" x 42" medium blue strips making eight sets of two strips. Press. Sew two strip sets together, making sure that the blue and white strips alternate. You will now have four sets of four pieced strips. Crosscut the sewn sets every 1½". Make 88 units.

2. Arrange in the checkerboard pattern and sew two sets of 26 units together to make the side borders. Sew two sets of 18 units together to make the top and bottom borders. Press as you sew.

3. Sew the top and bottom borders onto the large quarter-square star unit. Sew the side borders in place. Press. This completes the center unit.

Second Border

Sew a 2½" medium blue and cream print border to the top and bottom (48½") and sides (52½") of the center unit.

Wide Cornerstone Border

1. Sew the small cornerstone half quarter-square star blocks to the ends of two 9½" x 30½" gold/tan border strips to make the wide cornerstone border sections. Lay to the side.

2. Sew a 9½" x 30½" gold/tan border to the top and bottom of the center unit.

3. Sew the cornerstone borders to the sides of the center unit. Press.

Outer Border

Sew the 2½" x 42" medium blue print border strips together to fit the top, bottom, and sides of the table cover. Sew in place. Press.

Finishing the Table Cover

1. Sew the two backing fabric pieces together.

2. Layer and quilt as desired. In our example, the center star was outline stitched in the ditch. The checkerboard border was stitched on the diagonal both ways in the white blocks. The wide cornerstone border was diagonal stitched both ways. Both narrow blue borders and the blue backgrounds of the cornerstone blocks were meander stitched in coordinating thread.

3. Sew the binding strips end-to-end. Fold in half lengthwise, wrong sides together, and press. Sew the raw edge of the binding to the outer edge of the table cover. Fold the folded edge to the back and machine sew in place as this adds strength when machine washing.

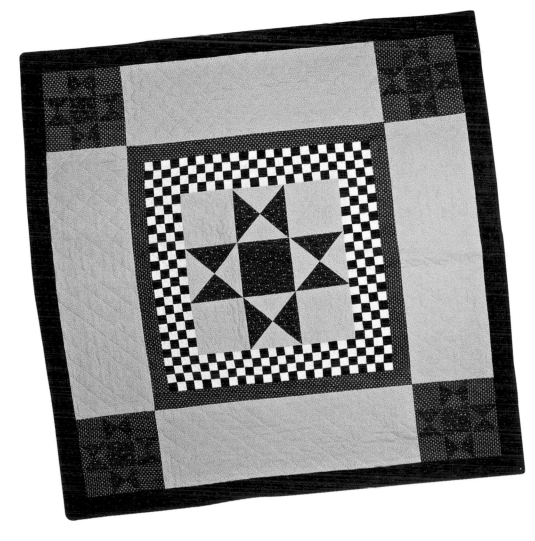

Spangled Star Banner

26½" x 48" Wall Quilt

Your visitors will feel welcome when they see this charming
wall quilt displayed inside or outside your door. The easily
made wall quilt is simply pieced with iron-on appliquéd stars.
The blanket stitch is used to highlight each star appliqué.

Preparation

1. Read all instructions before you begin.
2. Wash, dry, and press all fabrics.
3. Use ¼" seams throughout.
4. Press seam allowances in the direction that allows the seams to "lock" before continuing to build each block. Press all seams to the dark fabric when possible.
5. Cutting instructions are based on 42" wide fabrics.

Fabric and Tools Needed

- Fat quarter dark blue print for the Nine-Patch block
- Fat quarter medium blue print for the Nine-Patch block
- ⅓ yd. of each of the following fabrics:
  - ▶ light star print for the star appliqués and flag half-square triangle stripes
  - ▶ cream print for the flag half-square triangle stripes
  - ▶ medium red print for the flag half-square triangle stripes
  - ▶ medium light red print for the flag half-square triangle stripes
- ⅔ yd. dark blue star print for the border and binding
- 1½ yd. backing fabric
- 32" x 54" thin cotton batting
- ½ yd. iron-on fusible web
- One skein red embroidery floss
- 3 "O" rings for hanging, 1"
- Basic sewing supplies, rotary cutter, cutting mat, and see-through ruler
- 6½" square ruler (optional)

Cutting Instructions

From the dark blue fat quarter, cut
- (5) 5" squares

From the medium blue fat quarter, cut
- (4) 5" squares

From the light star print, cut
- (9) 5½" squares
- 8 stars

Trace the star appliqué onto the fusible web product. Peel off the back paper on the fusible web and iron it to the wrong side of the light star print. Cut out the eight star appliqués. Lay to the side.

From the cream print, cut
- (9) 5½" squares

From the medium red print, cut
- (12) 5½" squares

From the medium light red print, cut
- (12) 5½" squares

From the dark star print, cut
- (8) 2½" x 42" strips for the border and binding

Making the Blocks

1. To make the half-square triangles, draw a diagonal line across the wrong side of the medium light red print 5½" squares and the cream print 5½" squares.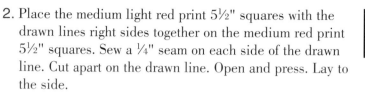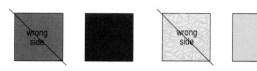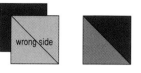

2. Place the medium light red print 5½" squares with the drawn lines right sides together on the medium red print 5½" squares. Sew a ¼" seam on each side of the drawn line. Cut apart on the drawn line. Open and press. Lay to the side.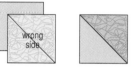

3. Place the cream print 5½" squares with the drawn lines right sides together on the 5½" light star print squares. Sew a ¼" seam on each side of the drawn line. Cut apart on the drawn line. Open and press. Lay to the side.

Building the Quilt

1. Sew a 5" dark blue square to both sides of two medium blue 5" squares. Press.

2. Sew two medium blue 5" squares to both sides of one 5" dark blue square. Press.

3. Sew the three rows of sewn blocks together to make the Nine-Patch block. Press. (See photo.)

4. Peel off the back paper on each of the star appliqués. Arrange the appliqués on the Nine-Patch block and iron in place.

5. Thread a needle with two strands of red embroidery floss. Stitch ¼" blanket stitches around each star. You can also machine stitch blanket stitches around each star if desired. Lay the Nine-Patch block to the side.

6. Refer to the Spangled Star Banner layout diagram often. Sew the dark red print side of each 5" half-square triangle to the medium red print side of a 5" half-square triangle. Sew two rows of seven half-square triangle blocks together. Sew one row of 10 half-square triangle blocks together. Press.

7. Refer to the Spangled Star Banner layout diagram often. Sew the light red print side of each 5" half-square triangle to the dark cream print side of each 5" half-square triangle. Sew one row of seven blocks together. Sew one row of 10 blocks together.

8. Sew the two rows of seven red half-square triangle blocks to the sides of the seven cream half-square triangle squares.

9. Sew the two rows of 10 half-square triangle squares together. Press.

10. Sew the Nine-Patch block to the top of the three half-square triangle block unit. Press.

11. Sew the remaining half-square triangle block unit to the right-hand side of the Nine-Patch block unit. Press.

12. Sew the 2½" dark star print border strips to the sides, top, and bottom.

13. Layer and quilt the Spangled Star Banner as desired. In the example shown, all areas were meander stitched in coordinating threads.

14. Sew the remaining 2½" binding strips end-to-end. Fold in half lengthwise and press.

15. Sew the raw edge of the binding to the outer edge of the quilt. Turn the folded edge of the binding to the back of the quilt and hand sew in place.

16. Attach three 1" rings to the top of the quilt for hanging.

Chapter 2

Cozy
Cottage Den

Wrap up and cuddle up in this cozy family room or den filled with flannel and homespun favorites.

The wonderful new flannel plaids, prints, and checks in rich forest colors add a masculine feeling to this collection.

The cuddle quilt combines the rag and chenille quilting techniques to make the handsome throw quilt.

Old-favorite quilt blocks, such as the Ohio Star, Bear Paw, and Flying Geese, are combined to make the other charming quilted pieces of this cozy collection.

Family

Cozy Cottage Cuddler

45" x 63" Chenille and Rag Throw

Set off any family room or den by making this wonderfully cozy cuddler quilt. This quilt drapes beautifully and would be stunning draped across a sofa or chair. The combination of two popular techniques, rag and chenille, is the basis of construction for the blocks and body on this throw. The quilt can be made larger by adding additional blocks on the sides, top, and bottom. Everyone will want to cuddle under this warm, masculine quilt.

Preparation

1. Read all instructions before you begin.
2. Do not wash fabric!
3. ½" seams are sewn "up" to connect squares!
4. Cutting instructions are based on 42" wide fabrics.

Fabric and Tools Needed

Choosing Fabrics

This quilt is constructed of flannel or homespun fabrics because these fabrics fray well. Four layers of fabric make up the body of the quilt. Choose a plaid fabric that can be sewn on a plaid line every ½" for the top layer. The two middle layers should be selections that show the color desired to complement the quilt top and back. The wrong side of the back layer of fabric will definitely show through, so choose a backing fabric that has a desired wrong side color or print. No batting is needed for this quilt. A short-bladed scissors is recommended for the clipping of all seams.

- 2⅔ yd. plaid flannel or homespun for the quilt top layer
- 2⅔ yd. each of two different flannel or homespun plaids or prints for the two center layers
- 3 yd. of a backing flannel or homespun fabric with a desired wrong side for the back layers and binding
- Short blade sharp scissors
- Wide package tape or sticky lint remover roller
- Basic sewing supplies, rotary cutter, cutting mat, and see-through ruler

Cutting Instructions

From 2⅔ yd. of each of the four fabrics, cut

- (9) 10" x 42" fabric strips

  Cut these strips into (35) 10" squares.

From the remaining ½ yd. of backing fabric, cut

- (6) 2½" x 42" strips for binding

Building the Blocks

The blocks are made by placing the back square right-side down on the tabletop. Layer the two middle fabric squares right-sides up and finish by placing the plaid square right-side up on the top of each square.

1. Layer each block as stated above.

2. Sew ½" seams diagonally on the plaid lines (or mark ½" lines if necessary.)

3. Carefully insert the scissors blade between the inside of the back layer and the three top layers between one seam line on the square. Cut through the three top layers. Do not cut through the bottom layer! Continue until each square has been cut between each seam line.

Chenille

Building the Quilt

1. Lay out the squares into seven rows of five blocks. You can see a chevron type of design as you turn the blocks in various directions.

2. When desired design is chosen, sew each row of blocks together sewing ½" seams UP!

3. Sew each row of the quilt together, again sewing ½" seams UP! Sew carefully over the seam intersections deciding to fold the seam in the same direction as you construct the center of the quilt.

Step 2

Finishing

1. Clip all seams every ¼" to the seam line.

2. Sew the binding strips end-to-end. Fold wrong sides together lengthwise and press.

3. Sew the raw edge of the binding around the outer edge of the quilt. Again, be careful sewing over the thick seam intersections on the quilt edge.

4. Fold the folded binding edge to the back of the quilt and machine or hand sew in place.

5. Place the quilt in the washing machine. Wash the quilt on the high, cold water setting. Remove any threads and lint that come loose from the quilt.

6. Place the quilt in the dryer and dry on a regular setting. Again remove the lint from the dryer. When the quilt is completely dry, shake it outside until most of the loose threads are gone.

7. Remove any additional lint by using a wide tape or sticky lint remover roller.

Bear's Den Coffee Table Runner

15" x 36" Table Runner

This table runner is made with some of the many delightful flannel prints that are now available. The ever-popular Bear Paw block is the basis for the design. Set a favorite decoy or basket of potpourri in the center of the runner to complete this cottage design.

Preparation

1. Read all instructions before you begin.
2. Wash and press all fabrics.
3. Use ¼" seams throughout.
4. Press seam allowances in the direction that allows the seam to "lock" before continuing to build each portion of each block. Press all seams to the dark fabric when possible.
5. Cutting instructions are based on 42" wide fabrics.

Fabrics and Tools Needed

- ½ yd. of the following fabrics:
  - ▶ border print
  - ▶ tan print
  - ▶ backing fabric
- ⅓ yd. rust print
- ⅔ yd. red check
- ½ yd. thin cotton batting

Cutting Instructions

From the border print, cut

- (4) 2½" x 42" strips

  From these strips, cut eight 2½" squares for Bear Paw block centers. The remaining 2½" strips are to be used for binding.

- (3) 1½" x 42" strips

  From these strips, cut two 1½" x 13½" strips for side borders, two 1½" x 34" strips for top and bottom borders, and four 1½" squares for lattice cornerstones.

From the rust print, cut

- (2) 2⅞" x 42" strips

  From these strips, cut (16) 2⅞" squares for the Bear Paw half-square triangles.

- (3) 1½" x 42" strips

  From these strips, cut (13) 1½" x 6½" sections for lattice.

From the red check, cut

- (1) 7¼" square for quarter-square center blocks
- (2) 2½" x 42" strips

  From these strips, cut eight 2½" x 4½" rectangles for Bear Paw block centers and eight 2½" squares for Bear Paw block centers.

- (4) 1½" squares for border cornerstone squares

From the tan print, cut

- (1) 7¼" square for quarter-square center blocks
- (2) 2⅞" x 42" strips

  From these strips, cut (16) 2⅞" squares for Bear Paw half-square triangles.

- (1) 2½" x 42" strip

  From this strip, cut (8) 2½" squares for the Bear Paw blocks.

Building the Blocks

Bear Paw Blocks – Make Eight

1. Place the 2½" red check squares right sides together on the 2½" border print squares. Sew together. Open and press.

2. Place the 2½" x 4½" red check rectangles right sides together on the above sewn squares. Sew together. Open and press.

3. Draw a diagonal line across the wrong side of the 2⅞" tan print squares. Place the squares with the drawn lines right sides together on the rust print 2⅞" squares. Sew a ¼" seam on each side of the drawn line. Cut on the drawn line. Open and press.

4. Lay out each block as shown. Sew two sets of half-square triangle squares together. Press. Sew a 2½" tan print square to the end of one of the half-square triangle sets. Press.

5. Sew the Bear Paw block together as shown.

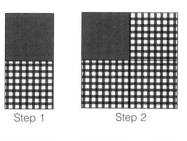

Step 1   Step 2

Step 3

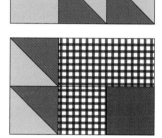

Step 4

Step 5

Quarter-Square Triangle Blocks – Make Two

1. Draw a diagonal line across the wrong side on the 7¼" tan print square.

2. Place the tan print squares with the drawn lines right sides together on the 7¼" red check square.

3. Sew a ¼" seam on each side of the drawn line. Cut on the drawn line. Open and press.

4. Draw a diagonal line across the wrong side of one of the half-square triangles. Place the squares with opposite fabrics touching right sides together.

5. Sew a ¼" seam on each side of the drawn line. Cut apart on the drawn line. Open and press.

Building the Table Runner

Refer to the Table Runner photo at right.

1. Sew a rust print 1½" x 6½" lattice section to the left-hand and right-hand side of the border print 1½" squares. Make four. Press.

2. Sew a Bear Paw block to each side of a 1½" x 6½" lattice section. Make four. Press.

3. Sew a red check side of each quarter-square triangle to each side of the remaining 1½" x 6½" lattice section.

4. Sew the rows of Bear Paw block sections together with the half-square triangle block section as shown to make the table runner center.

5. Sew the 1½" red check squares to the ends of the 1½" x 13½" border strips.

6. Sew the 1½" x 34" strips to the sides of the table runner. Sew the top and bottom borders in place.

Finishing

1. Layer and quilt the quilt as desired. In the sample shown, the Bear Paw blocks, quarter-square triangle blocks, and lattice strips were outline stitched in the ditch. A meandering pattern was stitched in the tan print areas.

2. Sew the binding strips end-to-end. Fold wrong sides together lengthwise. Press.

3. Sew the raw edge of the binding to the raw edge of the table runner; miter the corners as you sew on the binding.

4. Fold the folded edge of the binding to the back of the table runner and hand sew in place.

Lone Star Pillow

15" Pillow

The combination of the newest rich-colored flannels in plaids, prints, and marbles adds a warm finish to the favorite star block to create this cozy accent pillow.

Preparation

1. Read all instructions before you begin.
2. Wash and press all fabrics.
3. Use ¼" seams throughout.
4. Press seam allowances in the direction that allows them to "lock" before continuing to build each portion of each block. Press seams to the dark fabric when possible.
5. Cutting instructions are based on 42" wide fabrics.

Fabric and Tools Needed

- ½ yd. green flannel print for star block top and pillow backing
- Fat quarter or 18" x 22" of the following fabrics:
  - ▸ tan flannel tone-on-tone print for star block
  - ▸ dark green print for star block
  - ▸ muslin for star block backing
- Fat eighth or 9" x 22" gold plaid print for star block
- 18" square thin cotton batting
- (4) ¾" buttons
- 12" pillow form and polyester fiberfill stuffing
- Basic sewing supplies, rotary cutter, cutting mat, and see-through ruler

Cutting Instructions

From the ½ yd. of dark green flannel print, cut

- (2) 4⅞" squares for the half-square triangle corners
- (1) 4½" square for the star center square
- (2) 5¼" squares for the quarter-square triangles
- (1) 15½" square for the pillow back

From the tan print, cut

- (2) 5¼" squares for the quarter-square triangles

From the gold plaid print, cut

- (2) 4⅞" squares for the half-square triangle corners

From the fat quarter dark green print, cut

- (4) 2" x 22" strips

  From these strips, cut two 2" x 15½" border strips and two 2" x 12½" border strips.

Building the Pillow Top Squares

Half-Square Triangle Corners – Make Four

1. Draw a diagonal line across the wrong side of the 4⅞" gold squares.

2. Place the square with the drawn line right sides together on the 4⅞" dark green squares.

3. Sew a ¼" seam on each side of the drawn line. Open and press. Lay to the side.

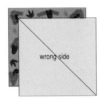

Quarter-Square Triangles – Make Four

1. Draw diagonal line across the wrong side of the 5¼" tan print squares.

2. Place the squares with the drawn lines right sides together on the dark green print 5¼" squares.

3. Sew a ¼" seam on each side of the drawn line. Cut apart on the drawn line. Open and press.

4. Place two of the squares right sides together with opposite fabrics touching. Draw a diagonal line across the wrong side of the top square. Repeat with the second set of squares.

5. Sew a ¼" seam on each side of the drawn line. Cut on the drawn line. Open and press.

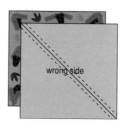

Building the Star Block Pillow Top

1. Lay out the star block as shown.

2. Sew three blocks together to make each row. Press.

3. Sew each row together to make the star block. Press.

4. Sew the 2" x 12½" border strips to the sides of the star block.

5. Sew the 2" x 15½" border strips to the top and bottom of the star block.

Finishing

1. Layer the batting between the star block pillow top and the muslin fabric.

2. Quilt as desired. Ours was meander stitched in the gold and tan fabrics.

3. Trim off the excess batting and muslin.

4. Place the pillow back fabric and the quilted star block pillow top right sides together. Sew around leaving a 10" opening on one side.

5. Sew the buttons on the center of each of the quarter-square triangle blocks on the star block pillow top.

6. Insert the 12" pillow form and place stuffing into the corners of the pillow until the pillow feels firm and looks smooth.

7. Hand sew the side opening shut.

Flying Geese Pillow

16" Pillow

Make this charming pillow by piecing together three sections of pieced blocks and units. The flying geese blocks form the center dividing unit. Leather buttons add a final rustic touch.

Preparation

1. Read all instructions before you begin.
2. Wash and press all fabrics.
3. Use ¼" seams throughout.
4. Press seam allowances in the direction that allows the seam to "lock" before continuing to build each portion of each block. Press all seams to the dark fabric when possible.
5. Cutting instructions are based on 42" wide fabric.

Fabric and Tools Needed

- Fat eighth or 9" x 22" of the following fabrics:
  - gold plaid flannel for pieced blocks
  - red check flannel for Flying Geese rectangles
  - tan print flannel for rectangles
- Fat quarter or 18" x 22" of the following fabrics:
  - rust print flannel for pieced blocks and Flying Geese
  - print or plaid flannel for backing
- ¼ yd. dark green print flannel for lattice, rectangles, and borders
- 18" muslin square
- 18" thin cotton batting square
- (9) ⅝" buttons
- 16" pillow form and polyester fiberfill stuffing

Cutting Instructions

From the gold plaid flannel, cut

- (1) 2⅞" x 22" strip

  From this strip, cut six 2⅞" squares for the pieced blocks.

From the rust flannel print, cut

- (2) 2½" x 22" strips

  From these strips, cut (14) 2½" squares for pieced blocks and Flying Geese.

- (1) 2⅞" x 22" strip

  From this strip, cut six 2⅞" squares for pieced blocks.

From the dark green print flannel, cut

- (1) 2½" x 42" strip

  From this strip, cut four 2½" x 6½" rectangles for top strip section and pieced section.

- (2) 1½" x 42" strips

  Cut these strips into two 1½" x 16½" border strips and two 1½" x 6½" border strips.

From the red check flannel, cut

- (1) 2½" x 22" strip

  From this strip, cut four 2½" x 4½" rectangles.

From the tan print flannel, cut

- (1) 2½" x 22" strip

  From this strip, cut two 2½" x 6½" rectangles.

- (1) 3½" x 22" strip

  From this strip, cut two 3½" x 6½" rectangles.

Building the Blocks

6½" Pieced Blocks – Make Two

1. Draw a diagonal line across the wrong side of the 2⅞" gold plaid squares.

2. Place the squares with the drawn lines right sides together on the 2⅞" rust print squares. Sew a ¼" seam on each side of the drawn line. Cut apart on the drawn line. Open and press. Make 12.

3. Lay out each block as shown, alternating the half-square triangles with the 2½" rust print squares.

4. Sew the three squares of each row together. Press.

5. Sew the three rows together. Press.

6. Sew the 6½" pieced blocks to the sides of a 2½" x 6½" dark green print flannel rectangle.

7. Sew a 1½" x 6½" dark green flannel print rectangle to each side and a 1½" x 16½" dark green flannel print border strip to the top and bottom to complete the bottom section of the pillow.

Flying Geese Rectangles – Make Four

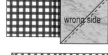

1. Draw a diagonal line across the wrong side of the remaining eight 2½" rust print squares.

2. Place a 2½" rust print square with the drawn line right sides together on the right-hand side of each of the four 2½" x 4½" red check rectangles. Sew on the drawn line.

3. Trim off the two back fabrics leaving a ¼" seam allowance. Open and press.

4. Repeat Step #2 on the left hand side of each rectangle.

5. Sew the Flying Geese rectangles together to make the pillow center section.

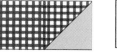

Pillow Top Row

1. Place two of the 2½" x 6½" dark green print flannel rectangles right sides together on the 2½" x 6½" tan print flannel rectangles. Sew along the long side. Open and press.

2. Sew the remaining 2½" x 6½" dark green print rectangle to the 3½" x 6½" tan print rectangle. Open and press.

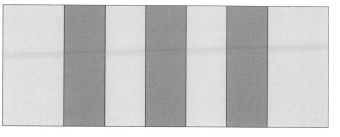

3. Sew the rectangles together starting with a 3½" x 6½" tan print rectangle and ending with the 3½" x 6½" tan print rectangle. See Pillow photo.

4. Sew the three sections of the pillow top together.

Finishing

1. Layer the batting between the pillow top and muslin back. Quilt as desired. The example shown was meander quilted in the tan, gold, and red check areas. Trim off any excess muslin and batting.

2. Place the pillow top and backing fabrics right sides together. Sew around leaving a 12" opening on one side. Attach the buttons.

3. Insert the pillow form and stuff the corners with the polyester fiberfill stuffing until the pillow is firm and smooth.

4. Hand sew the pillow opening shut.

Tall Tree Pillow

10" x 19" Accent Pillow

The shape, size, and design of this pillow
will add an interesting touch to the den. The
center panel is easily constructed by making
half-square triangle rectangle units. The pillow
is quick, easy, and fun to make.

Preparation

1. Read all instructions before you begin.
2. Wash and press all fabrics.
3. Use ¼" seams throughout.
4. Press seam allowances in the direction that allows the seam to "lock" before continuing to build each portion of each block. Press all seams to the dark fabric when possible.
5. Cutting instructions are based on 42" wide fabrics.

Fabrics and Tools Needed

- Fat eighth or 9" x 22" tan tone-on-tone print for background
- Fat quarter or 18" x 22" of the following fabrics:
  - ▶ dark green print for tree and border
  - ▶ border print for border
  - ▶ print for backing
- Scrap dark brown flannel for tree trunk
- 14" x 22" muslin
- 14" x 22" thin cotton batting
- Polyester fiberfill stuffing
- Basic sewing supplies, rotary cutter, cutting mat, and see-through ruler

Cutting Instructions

From the tan tone-on-tone print flannel, cut

- ■ (3) 2½" x 22" strips

  From these strips, cut (12) 2½" x 3½" rectangles and two 2½" x 3" rectangles for the tree background.

From the dark brown flannel scrap, cut

- ■ (1) 1½" x 2½" rectangle for the tree trunk

From the dark green flannel print, cut

- ■ (2) 2½" x 22" strips

  From these strips, cut (12) 2½" squares.

- ■ (3) 1" x 22" strips

  From these strips, cut two 1" x 14½" inner border strips and two 1" x 7½" inner border strips.

From the border print, cut

- ■ (2) 2½" x 15½" border strips
- ■ (2) 2½" x 11" border strips

Building the Pillow

1. Draw a diagonal line across all of the 2½" dark green flannel squares.

2. Place six of the squares with drawn lines right sides together on the left-hand side of the 2½" x 3½" tan tone-on-tone flannel rectangles. Sew on the drawn line. Trim off the back fabrics leaving a ¼" seam allowance. Open and press.

3. Place the remaining six squares with drawn lines on the right-hand side of the rectangles. Repeat as in Step 2.

4. Place the green fabric edges right sides together and sew the pairs together to equal six units. Referring to the photo, assemble the six units to make the tree top section. Press.

5. Sew a 2½" x 3" tan tone-on-tone flannel rectangle to each side of the 1½" x 2½" rectangle to make the tree trunk section.

6. Sew the tree trunk section to the bottom of the tree top section. Press.

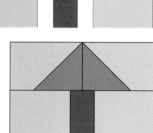

7. Sew a 1" x 14½" dark green border strip to the sides of the center panel. Sew a 1" x 7½" dark green border strip to the top and bottom of the center pillow panel. Press.

8. Sew a 2½" x 15½" border print strip to both sides of the pillow center. Sew a 2½" x 11" border print strip to the top and bottom of the pillow. Press.

Masculine

Finishing

1. Layer the pillow top on top of the thin batting and muslin fabric. Quilt as desired. The example shown was meander quilted in the tan background areas and in the border print. Trim off the excess muslin fabric and batting.

2. Place the pillow top and backing fabric right sides together. Sew around leaving an 8" opening on one side.

3. Stuff the pillow firmly. Hand sew the opening shut.

Chapter 3

Cherry Berry Kitchen

C ome on in and sit awhile. This charming kitchen is ever so inviting decorated with the cherry berry basket quilted place mats, appliquéd valances, towels, trivet, potholders, and quilted tote centerpiece. The high contrast fabrics add a crisp, clean touch to the checkerboard.

Inviting

Cherry Berry Basket Place Mats

13½" x 18" Pieced and Quilted Place Mats

These fun pieced and appliquéd place mats add definite charm to any meal. The easy iron-on method of appliqué is used to attach the leaves, cherries, and basket handles. The instructions and fabrics needed are given to make four place mats. Make as many as you need.

Preparation

1. Read all instructions before you begin.
2. Wash and press all fabrics.
3. Use ¼" seams throughout.
4. Press seam allowances in the direction that allows them to "lock" before continuing to build each portion of each block. Press all seams to the dark fabric when possible.
5. Cutting instructions are based on 42" wide fabrics.

Fabrics and Tools Needed

- ¾ yd. yellow print
- 1¾ yd. blue print
- ⅓ yd. cream print
- ⅓ yd. red check
- ⅛ yd. or scraps of dark red and green prints
- ½ yd. iron-on fusible web
- 1 yd. thin cotton batting
- Basic sewing supplies, rotary cutter, cutting mat, and see through ruler

Cutting Instructions

From the yellow print, cut

- (4) 5½" x 14½" rectangles for the center panel background
- (1) 3½" x 42" strip

    From this strip, cut eight 3½" x 4½" rectangles for bottom background sections.
- (1) 3¼" x 42" strip

    From this strip, cut four 3¼" squares for quarter-square triangles and four 2⅞" squares for half-square triangles.
- (1) 2½" x 42" strip

    From this strip, cut eight 2½" squares for bottom background sections.

From the blue print, cut

- (2) 17" x 42" strips

    From these strips, cut four 17" x 21" rectangles for place mat backings.
- (6) 2½" x 42" strips

    From two of these strips, cut four 2½" x 4½" rectangles for basket tops and (16) 2½" squares for border cornerstones.

    The remaining 2½" strips are binding strips.
- (1) 3¼" x 42" strip

    From this strip, cut four 3¼" squares for quarter-square triangles.

    Cut the remainder of the 3¼" strip into a 2⅞" strip and cut this into four 2⅞" squares for the half-square triangles.

    From the remaining blue print fabric, cut four basket handle appliqués from iron-on fused fabric.

From the cream print, cut

- (7) 1½" x 42" strips for the checkerboard border

From the red check, cut

- (7) 1½" x 42" strips for the checkerboard border

From the dark red print, cut

- 16 cherry appliqués from iron-on fused fabric

From the green print, cut

- 16 leaf appliqués from iron-on fused fabric

From the thin cotton batting, cut

- (4) 17" x 21" rectangles

Building the Center Panel

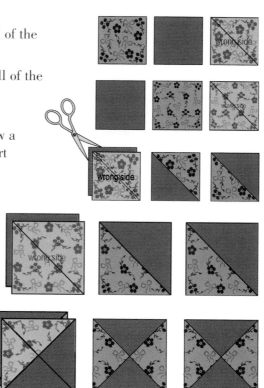

1. Draw a diagonal line across the wrong side on all of the 2⅞" yellow print squares.

2. Draw a diagonal line across the wrong sides on all of the 3¼" yellow print squares.

3. Place the 2⅞" squares with the drawn lines right sides together on the blue print 2⅞" squares. Sew a ¼" seam on each side of the drawn line. Cut apart on the drawn line. Open and press.

4. Place the 3¼" yellow print squares with drawn lines right sides together on the 3¼" blue print squares. Sew a ¼" seam on each side of the drawn line. Cut apart on the drawn line. Open and press. Lay to the side.

5. Draw another diagonal line across the wrong side on four of the sewn squares. Place the sewn squares right sides together with opposite fabrics touching. Sew a ¼" seam on each side of the drawn line. Cut apart on the drawn line. Make eight quarter-square squares. Open and press.

6. To make the basket bottom unit, sew the yellow sides of two quarter-square squares together. Open and press.

7. Sew the 2½" x 4½" blue print rectangle to the top of the basket bottom units.

8. Sew a 2½" square to the yellow print side of the half-square triangle squares from Step 1.

9. Referring to the diagram below, sew the 4½" side of the yellow print rectangle to the right-hand side on one of the half-square triangle squares and 2½" yellow print square units.

10. Repeat on the left hand side. Make four of each.

11. Sew the three units together to make the bottom of the center panel.

12. Sew the 5½" x 14½" yellow print rectangle to the top of each of the center panels.

Checkerboard Border

1. Sew a 1½" x 42" red check strip to a 1½" x 42" cream print strip. Repeat this process on all seven strips.

2. Crosscut each strip set into 1½" sections.

3. Place opposite fabrics right sides together in pairs. Sew together. Make 88 Four-Patch squares.

4. Sew seven Four-Patch squares together to make the top and bottom borders (14 crosscuts).

5. Sew four Four-Patch squares together. Add one crosscut to the end to total nine crosscuts for each side border.

6. Sew a 2½" blue print square to each end of the nine crosscut checkerboard side borders.

7. Sew the top and bottom checkerboard borders in place. Press.

8. Sew the side checkerboard borders in place. Press.

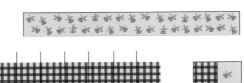

Appliqués

1. Trace the appliqués onto the iron-on fusible web as stated on the pattern pieces. Trace the shapes in groups, leaving ½" between each shape.

2. Cut around the shapes allowing a little excess.

3. Peel off the paper backing on the fusible web.

4. Iron the fusible web to the wrong side of the appliqué fabric you are using. Cut out each appliqué.

5. Peel off the paper backing and arrange the appliqués as desired. Press in place.

6. Sew a decorative stitch around each appliqué.

Finishing

1. Layer and quilt each place mat. The model was meander quilted everywhere except over the basket and cherry appliqués.

2. Trim off any excess batting and backing fabric.

3. Fold each 2½" x 42" blue print strip wrong sides together lengthwise. Press.

4. Sew the raw edge of the binding to the outer edge of the place mat, mitering the corner as you go.

5. Fold the folded edge of the binding to the back and hand sew or machine sew in place.

Country

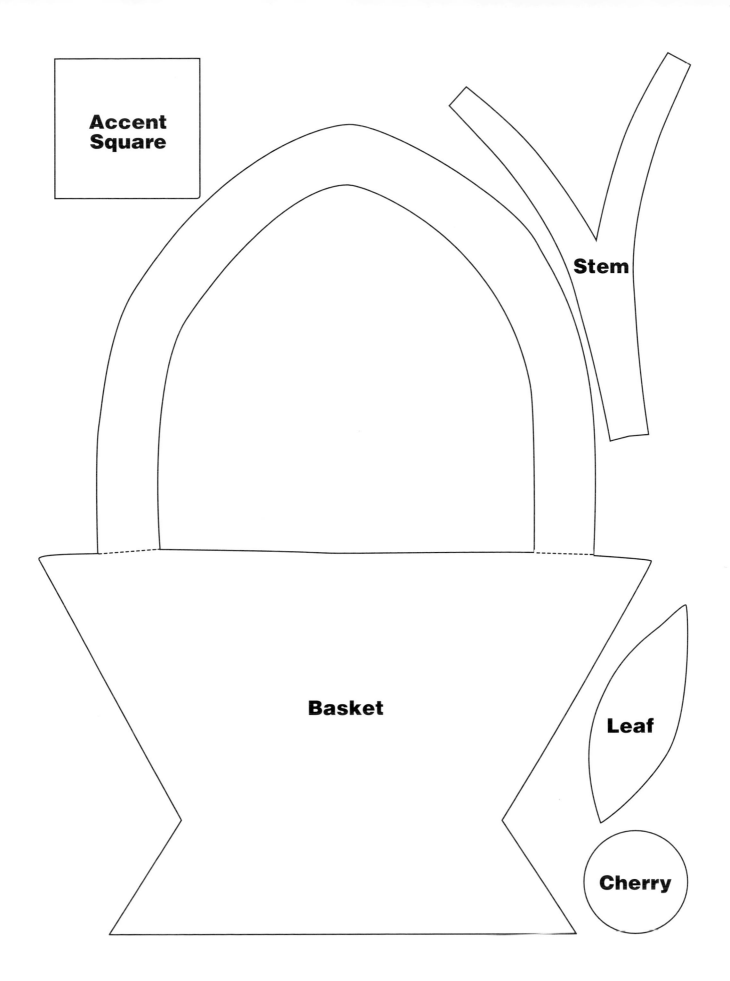

Accent Square

Stem

Basket

Leaf

Cherry

Cherry Berry Valances

Two 14" x 40" Valances

Your windows will shine when dressed in these great appliquéd and pieced valances. A Thermalsuede® lining is recommended to protect the fabrics from fading. The crosscut checkerboard border and the iron-on cherry basket appliqués add the cottage charm to these fun valances. Hang them alone or double hang them in front of plain or lace panels to soften the room.

Preparation

1. Read all instructions before you begin.
2. Wash and press the top fabrics (but not the lining).
3. Use ¼" seams throughout.
4. Press seam allowances in the direction that allows the seam to "lock" before continuing to build each portion of each block. Press seams to the dark fabric when possible.
5. Cutting instructions are based on 42" wide fabrics.

Fabrics and Tools Needed

- ⅔ yd. yellow print
- 1 yd. blue print
- ¼ yd. red check print
- ¼ yd. cream print
- ⅛ yd. or scrap green print and red prints
- ¾ yd. iron-on fusible web
- ⅔ yd. Roclon® Thermalsuede® drapery lining
- Basic sewing supplies, rotary cutter, cutting mat, and see-through ruler

Cutting Instructions

From the yellow print, cut

- (2) 10" x 42" fabric strips for the background pieces

  From the remaining yellow print, trace and cut six basket accent squares (page 77).

From the blue print fabric, cut

- (2) 7½" x 42" strips for the basket appliqués

  From these strips, cut six basket appliqués (page 77) from iron-on fused fabrics.

- (3) 4½" x 42" strips

  From these strips, cut (12) 4½" x 6½" rectangles for the valance tabs.

From the red check, cut

- (3) 1½" x 42" strips

From the cream print, cut

- (3) 1½" x 42" strips

From the red and green scrap fabrics, cut

- 24 leaf and 24 cherry appliqués (page 77) from iron-on fused fabrics

From the Thermalsuede® lining, cut

- (2) 9¾" x 42" strips

Making the Cherry Berry Basket Valances

1. Trace the basket, cherries, and leaf appliqués on the iron-on fusible web as stated.

2. Cut around each group of traced patterns. Peel off the paper backing and iron the appliqué shapes to the wrong side of the appliqué fabrics. Cut out each appliqué. Lay to the side.

3. Fold and press the yellow print fabric strips to make the placements for the three baskets on each valance.

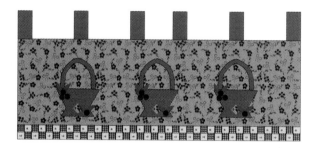

4. Peel off the paper backing on each appliqué shape. Refer to the color photo and place the appliqués on the pressed lines. Press in place. Machine sew a decorative or straight stitch around each appliqué to hold in place.

5. Fold the 4½" x 42" blue print fabric strips wrong sides together and sew the long seam on each strip.

6. Cut the sewn strips into (12) 6½" lengths. Turn right side out and press with the seam to the back center on each tab.

7. Fold the tabs in half with the seam to the inside. Measure equal distance between each tab and pin the tab raw edges to the top edge of the valance front. Place the pins about an inch below the top edge so that they are not in the way when the lining is attached.

8. Place the valance fronts and linings right sides together. (The lining is ¼" smaller than the front of the valance in order that the top and bottom of the valance fall to the back and the lining cannot be seen on the front edges.) Sew the long top and bottom seams.

9. Fold the side edges in ¼" and sew in place.

10. Slip the valances onto the curtain rod. Arrange folds so that the baskets come to the front.

Cherry Berry Potholders

Two 8" x 8" Potholders

    Layer up the batting, add a little fabric and a charming cherry appliqué, and you have fun and functional quilted potholders. These potholders are easy to make and can be washed as much as needed. The fabrics and instructions are for two potholders.

Preparation

1. Read all instructions before you begin.
2. Wash and press all fabrics.
3. Use ¼" seams throughout.
4. Cutting instructions are based on 42" wide fabrics.

Fabric and tools needed

- ¼ yd. yellow print
- ¼ yd. red check print
- ⅔ yd. thin cotton batting
- Fat eighth or scraps of green print, dark red print, and tan print
- ⅛ yd. iron-on fusible web
- Basic sewing supplies, rotary cutter, cutting mat, and see-through ruler

Cutting Instructions

From the yellow print, cut

- (1) 8" x 42" strip

  From this strip, cut four 8" squares for potholder tops and backs.

From the red check print, cut

- (2) 2½" x 42" strips for binding and hanging loops

From the dark red print, cut

- Six cherry appliqués (page 77) from the iron-on fused fabrics

From the green print, cut

- Four leaf appliqués (page 77) from the iron-on fused fabrics

From the tan print, cut

- Two stem appliqués (page 77) from the iron-on fused fabrics

From the thin cotton batting, cut

- (6) 8" squares

Making the Potholders

1. Trace the appliqués as needed on the iron-on fusible web.
2. Cut out each appliqué and peel off the paper back.
3. Place the appliqués on the potholder front.
4. Sew around each appliqué using a decorative stitch.
5. Layer the batting squares on the wrong side of an 8" yellow print square and the appliquéd top.
6. Pin all layers together. Sew a straight stitch around the appliqués to quilt all of the layers together.
7. Fold the two 2½" x 42" red check fabric strips wrong sides together and press lengthwise.
8. Sew the raw edge of the binding to the raw edge of the potholder mitering the edges as you sew.
9. Fold and sew the excess binding in half to make a ⅜" x 6" hanging loop. Sew the ends of the loop to the top corner on each potholder to finish.

Fun

Cherry Berry Trivet

8" Scented Trivet

Smell the wonderful aroma of cinnamon and spice when you place a hot tea kettle or pan on this scented trivet. The trivet is filled with a removable pouch that contains rice and a cinnamon and spice potpourri. Another piece to fill your Cottage Cherry Berry Kitchen!

Preparation

1. Read all instructions before you begin.
2. Wash and press all fabrics.
3. Use ¼" seams throughout.
4. Cutting instructions are based on 42" wide fabrics.

Fabric and Tools Needed

- Fat quarter or 18" x 22" blue print
- Two 9" squares muslin or scrap fabrics
- ⅛" yd. yellow print
- Fat eighth or scraps of dark red print, green print, and tan print
- ⅛ yd. or scrap iron-on fusible web
- ¼ yd. thin cotton batting
- One cup raw rice
- One envelope cinnamon spice potpourri

Cutting Instructions

From the blue print, cut

- (1) 8½" square for the front on the trivet
- (2) 5" x 8½" rectangles for the trivet back

From the muslin or scrap 9" squares, cut

- (2) 8¼" squares

From the yellow print, cut

- (1) 2½" x 42" strip for binding

From the ⅛ yd. or scrap appliqué fabrics, cut

- Three cherry, two leaf, and one stem appliqué (page 77) from iron-on fused fabrics

From the thin cotton batting, cut

- (2) 8½" squares
- (4) 4½" x 8½" rectangles

Making the Trivet

1. Place the two 8¼" muslin or scrap fabric squares right sides together. Sew around leaving a 4" opening on one side.

2. Turn right side out. Pour the rice and potpourri into the opening. Lay the potpourri pouch on a table top and spread out the potpourri so that the pouch remains flat. Do not over-fill. Sew the opening shut.

3. Trace the cherry, stem, and leaf appliqué shapes on the iron-on fusible web. Cut out each appliqué. Peel off the paper and iron the appliqué onto the center of the 8½" blue print square. Sew each appliqué shape in place using a decorative stitch.

4. Place the two layers of batting under the trivet top and sew around the appliqué to quilt all layers together. Continue to quilt the trivet top.

5. Layer two of the 4½" x 8½" batting pieces behind each of the blue print backing fabrics. Quilt the layers together.

6. Fold the 2½" x 42" yellow print strips wrong sides together and press. Sew the raw edge of the binding to one 8½" side on each of the 4½" x 8½" rectangle trivet backs.

7. Overlap the ends of the bound edges and top sew 1" on each end.

8. Place the trivet top and back wrong sides together. Sew the remaining binding around the trivet.

9. Insert the potpourri pouch into the back opening. Shake the potpourri around until it is as flat as possible.

Cherry Berry Basket Towels

Two 18" x 28" Kitchen Hand Towels

Decorated towels are becoming one of the most popular home décor items in catalogs and department stores. These towels are easily made by adding the appliqués to pre-purchased homespun towels. Simply iron on the appliqués, stitch around them, and enjoy your new towels in no time at all.

Preparation

1. Read all instructions before you begin.
2. Wash and press all appliqué fabrics and towels.
3. Cutting instructions are based on 42" wide fabrics.

Fabric and Tools Needed

- Fat eighth or ¼ yd. blue print
- Scrap pieces of yellow print, dark red print, and green print
- ½ yd. iron-on fusible web
- Basic sewing supplies, rotary cutter, cutting mat, and see-through ruler

Cutting Instructions

From the blue print, trace and cut out

- Two basket appliqués (page 77) from the iron-on fused fabrics

From the yellow print, trace and cut out

- Two basket square accent appliqués (page 77) from the iron-on fused fabrics

From the dark red print, trace and cut out

- Four cherry appliqués (page 77) from the iron-on fused fabrics

From the green print, trace and cut out

- Four leaf appliqués (page 77) from the iron-on fused fabrics

Making the Towels

1. Peel off the paper backing from each appliqué.
2. Arrange each appliqué as shown in the photo.
3. Iron in place.
4. Sew a decorative stitch around each appliqué to finish.

Cherry Berry Basket Towels •87•

Building the Quilted Tote Bag Centerpiece

1. Place the red check and cream print fabric strips right sides together and sew together along the long edge.

2. Open and press.

3. Crosscut the strip unit into (24) 1½" sections.

4. Lay out two sets of seven crosscut sections and two sets of five crosscut sections in a checkerboard design. Sew the pieces of each section together.

5. Sew a 7½" x 9½" yellow print rectangle to the top of each of the seven-pieced checkerboard borders. Press.

6. Sew a 5½" x 9½" yellow print rectangle to the top of each of the five-pieced checkerboard borders. Press.

7. Place the batting pieces between the muslin back and front panels as well as the bottom panel.

8. Quilt as desired. Our example was meander quilted over the entire surface.

9. Trim off the excess muslin and batting.

Building the Tote Lining

1. Place a 5½" x 11½" blue print rectangle side unit right sides together on one side of a 7½" x 11½" rectangle unit. Sew the 11½" seam.

2. Sew a side of the remaining 7½" x 11½" blue print rectangle to the side of the remaining 5½" x 11½" side unit. Sew one side of the remaining panel in place.

3. Sew the bottom unit by placing the 5½" side of the bottom right sides together on the 5½" edge of the front panel. Sew in place.

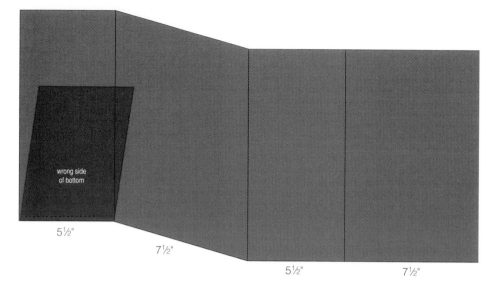

Leave the needle inserted; rotate and sew the side seam;

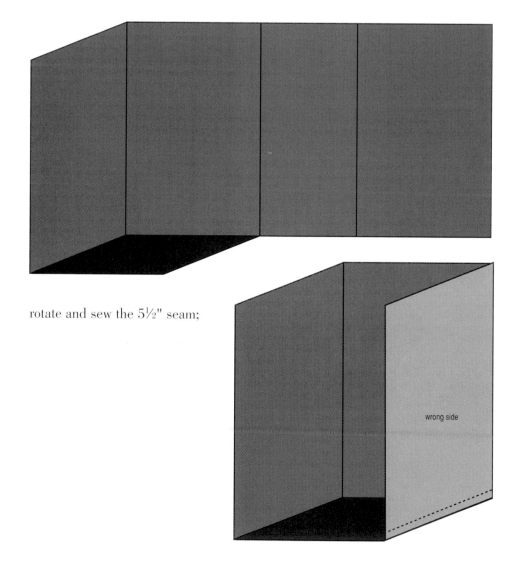

rotate and sew the 5½" seam;

again leave the needle down; rotate and sew the remaining seam to the bottom of the tote. Sew the side seam.

4. Repeat this process to sew the quilted pieces of the tote together. This will make the outside of the tote.

5. Turn right side out.

6. Insert the lining. Fold the lining to the outside top and stitch in place.

7. Insert a pint or quart jar to hold a bouquet or kitchen utensils.

8. Fold a large cuff of the lining to the outside to fit the pint jar.

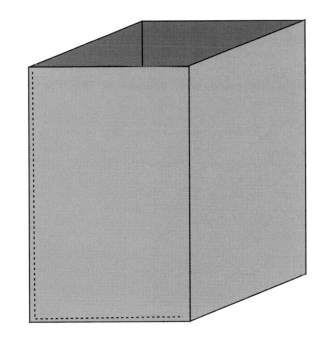

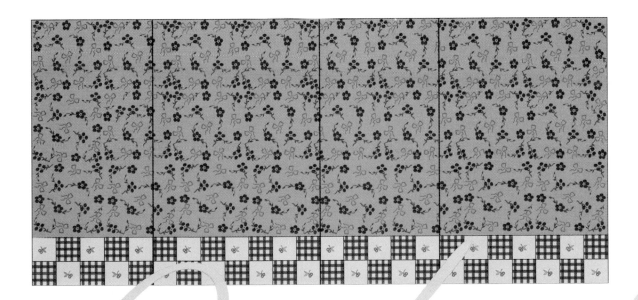

Chapter 4

Bed of Roses Bedroom

Build your own rose garden in your favorite bedroom. The beautiful, bright hues add a touch of romantic charm to this room.

Basic pieced blocks, iron-on appliques, and lovely handwork are the featured techniques.

A vintage feeling is added with the yo-yo pillow and hand-embroidered picture.

The garden palette is refreshing and upbeat while the overall pattern lends an old-fashioned feeling to this inviting setting.

Bed of Roses Quilt

92" x 102" Queen Quilt

This beautiful patchwork quilt is constructed of Windowpane and Four-Patch blocks. The iron-on scallop appliqués accent the wide border. The stitch in the ditch and free-form quilting add a final cottage touch to this wonderful quilt.

Preparation

1. Read all instructions before you begin.
2. Wash and press all fabrics.
3. Use ¼" seams throughout.
4. Press seam allowances in the direction that allows the seam to "lock" before continuing to build each block portion of each block. Press seams to the dark fabric when possible.
5. Cutting instructions are based on 42" wide fabrics.

Fabrics and Tools Needed

- ⅔ yd. large rose-pink floral print for Windowpane blocks and first border cornerstones
- 1⅓ yd. large blue floral print for Windowpane blocks and first border
- 2¼ yd. large yellow floral print for Windowpane blocks and scallop appliqués
- 1¾ yd. rose-pink tone-on-tone print for Four-Patch blocks
- 1¾ yd. small yellow print for Four-Patch blocks
- 2¼ yd. green print for Windowpane block borders
- 3 yd. blue tone-on-tone print for wide border and binding
- 3 yd. iron-on fusible light-weight interfacing
- Threads to match fabrics
- 9 yd. small print for backing
- Queen size thin cotton batting
- Basic sewing supplies, rotary cutter, cutting mat, and see-through ruler

Cutting Instructions

From the large rose-pink floral print, cut

- (4) 5" x 42" strips

  From these strips, cut (28) 5" squares for Windowpane blocks.

- (4) 2½" squares for first border cornerstones

From the large blue floral print, cut

- (4) 5" x 42" strips

  From these strips, cut (28) 5" squares for Windowpane blocks.

- (8) 2½" x 44" strips for first border

From the large yellow floral print, cut

- (4) 5" x 42" strips

  From these strips, cut (28) 5" squares for Windowpane blocks.

- (8) 6" x 42" strips

  From these strips, cut (30) side scallop appliqués and four corner scallop appliqués as stated.

From the rose-pink tone-on-tone print, cut

- (16) 3½" x 42" strips for Four-Patch blocks

From the small yellow print, cut

- (16) 3½" x 42" strips for the Four-Patch blocks

From the light-weight iron-on fusible interfacing, cut

- 30 side scallop appliqués and four corner scallop appliqués as stated

From the small green print, cut

- (28) 1½" x 42" strips

  From these strips, cut (168) 1½" x 5" segments.

- (21) 1½" x 42" strips

  From these strips, cut (168) 1½" x 6½" segments.

From the blue tone-on-tone print, cut

- (9) 8½" x 42" strips for the outer border
- (10) 2½" x 42" strips for the binding

Beautiful

Building the Blocks

Windowpane Blocks –
Make 28 of Each Color

1. Sew a 1½" x 5" light green segment to the left-hand and right-hand sides of each 5" square (large rose, blue, and yellow florals). Press.

2. Sew a 1½" x 6½" light green segment to the top and bottom of each square. Press and lay to the side.

Four Patch Blocks –
Make 84

These blocks are easily constructed using the strip piecing method as shown in the General Instructions and Tools Chapter (page 18).

1. Place a 3½" x 42" rose-pink tone-on-tone strip right sides together on a 3½" x 42" small yellow print strip. Sew together. Open and press. Continue until 16 pairs of strips are sewn together. Press.

2. Crosscut each sewn strip into 3½" segments.

3. Place two of the 3½" segments with opposite fabrics touching, right-sides together. Sew together. Open and press. Continue sewing the Four-Patch blocks together to make the 84 blocks needed.

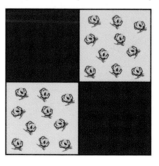

Building the Quilt

1. Refer to the project photo (page 100) often.

2. Lay out each row of the quilt as shown. Sew the first row of 12 blocks together starting with a yellow print Windowpane block and ending with a Four-Patch block.

3. Sew 14 rows of 12 blocks together as shown. Press each seam before sewing on an additional row of blocks.

4. Sew the sides, top, and bottom first borders onto the quilt center. (See First Border below.)

5. Measure the quilt across and up and down for exact measurements. Cut the top and bottom outer borders (tone-on-tone blue print) to fit across the top and bottom of the quilt (approximately 8½" x 82½")*. Cut the side borders to fit (approximately 8½" x 111½")*.

6. Place the iron-on fusible interfacing, web side out, on top of the right side on each of the large yellow floral print scallops and corner scallops. Sew around the entire scallop shape using a ¼" seam allowance.

7. Clip all around and then cut a 2" to 3" slit in the center of the web. Turn right side out making sure all seam areas are smooth. Press each scallop. This will attach the interfacing for a perfect finish.

8. Lay out the scallops on the borders so that there is the same distance above, below, and side-to-side.

9. Pin the scallops in place. Sew the scallops in place using a decorative stitch and matching thread. A large blanket stitch was used on the model.

10. Sew the borders onto the quilt. Press.

First Border

1. Sew the 2½" x 42" large blue floral print strips together to make the first border.

2. From the sewn border strips, cut two 2½" x 91½" sections for the side borders. Cut two 2½" x 78½" sections for the top and bottom borders.

3. Sew the 2½" large rose-pink floral squares to the ends of the 78½" top and bottom first border sections. Press.

The border measurements could change slightly as ¼" seams vary from machine to machine. Always measure your quilt to find exact measurements for the borders.

Finishing the Quilt

1. Cut the nine yards of backing fabric into three 3-yd. pieces. Sew the three pieces together to make the quilt backing.

2. Layer and quilt as desired. The model was quilted using a free-form quilted rose in the Windowpane blocks; stipple quilting was used on the Four-Patch blocks; and a medium meander quilting technique was used on the outer border.

3. Sew the 2½" blue tone-on-tone binding strips end-to-end. Fold in half lengthwise and press.

4. Sew the raw edge of the binding to the outer edge of the quilt. Miter the corners as you attach the binding. Fold the folded edge of the binding to the back and hand or machine stitch in place.

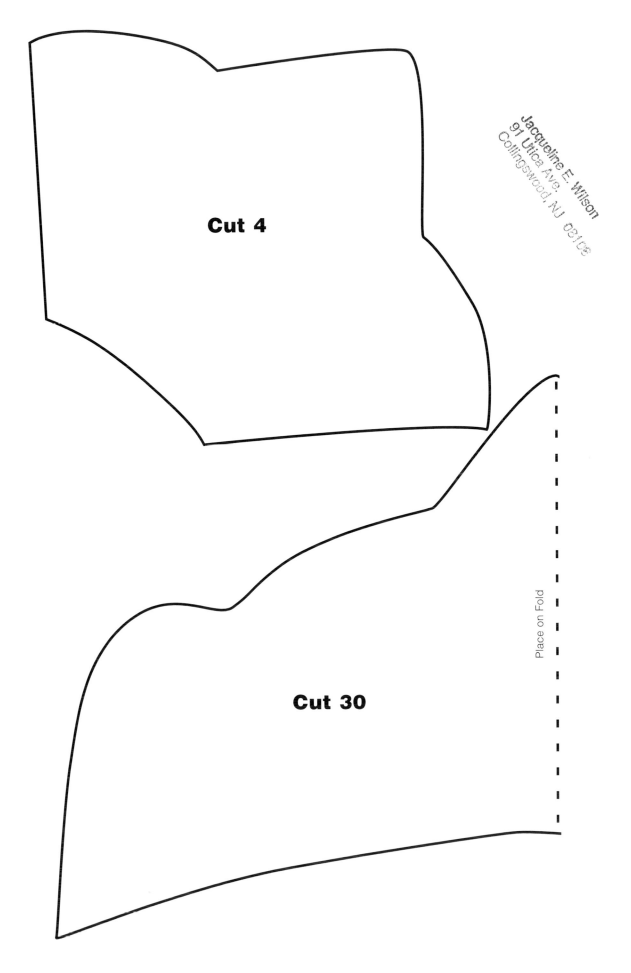

Cut 4

Place on Fold

Cut 30

Bed of Roses Bed Skirt

Full-Size Pleated Bed Skirt

A full bed skirt always adds a finishing touch to the complete
bed collection. By adding a wide pleated ruffle to the bottom of
a purchased bed skirt, a full pleated bed skirt can be finished
in no time at all.

Preparation

1. Read all instructions before you begin.
2. Wash and press all fabrics.
3. Use ¼" seams throughout.
4. Press all seams.
5. Cutting instructions are based on 42" wide fabric.

Fabrics and Tools Needed

■ 2½ yd. green check fabric
■ Purchased full-size ruffled bed skirt
■ Basic sewing supplies, rotary cutter, cutting mat, and see-through ruler

Cutting Instructions

From the green check fabric, cut

■ (11) 8" strips

Sewing Instructions

1. Sew the (11) 8" fabric strips end-to-end.
2. Fold one long edge under ¼" and sew a hem.
3. Fold the top edge of the pieced fabric strips under ½" and sew in place the entire length.
4. Fold the ½" edge of the fabric strips under ½" every 1½" to make the pleats.

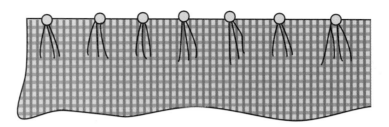

5. Place the bottom edge of the pleated ruffle ¼" over the hemmed edge on the bed skirt. Sew the pleated edge down, sewing over the pleated stitch line.
6. Fold the end of the pleated ruffle under ¼" and sew to the bed skirt to finish.

Romance

Bed of Roses Table Topper

42" Square Quilted Topper

This charming table topper adds another cottage accent to the bedroom of your choice. The bold colors remind one of a beautiful summer day. The star blocks are always a favorite.

Preparation

1. Read all instructions before you begin.
2. Wash and press all fabrics.
3. Use ¼" seams throughout.
4. Press seam allowances in the direction that allows the seam to "lock" before continuing to build each portion of each block. Press all seams to the dark fabric when possible.
5. Cutting instructions are based on 42" wide fabrics.

Fabrics and Tools Needed

- ⅔ yd. large yellow floral print
- 1 yd. small yellow floral print
- 1½ yd. rose-pink tone-on-tone print
- ⅓ yd. small light green print
- Fat quarter small dark green print
- ⅛ yd. light blue print
- 1¼ yd. backing fabric
- 1¼ yd. thin cotton batting

Cutting Instructions

From the large yellow print, cut

- (3) 6½" x 42" strips

  From these strips, cut (13) 6½" squares for center panel square and border squares.

- (4) 3⅞" squares for half-square triangle Four-Patch blocks

From the small yellow floral print, cut

- (3) 6½" x 42" strips

  From these strips, cut (16) 6½" squares for star blocks.

- (1) 2½" x 42" strip

  From this strip, cut (2) 2½" x 21" strips for the checkerboard squares.

- (1) 3¼" x 42" strip

  From this strip, cut (8) 3½" squares for the half-square triangle blocks.

From the rose-pink tone-on-tone print, cut

- (2) 6½" x 42" strips

  From these strips, cut (8) 6½" squares for star block centers.

- (2) 7¼" x 42" strips

  From these strips, cut (8) 7¼" squares for the Four-Patch star point squares.

- (5) 2½" x 42" strips for binding

From the small dark green print fat quarter, cut

- (2) 2½" x 22" strips for Four-Patch blocks

From the small light green print, cut

- (3) 3½" x 42" strips

  From these strips cut (32) 3½" squares for star block centers.

From the light blue print, cut

- (1) 3⅞" x 42" strip

  From this strip, cut (4) 3⅞" squares.

Bright

Building the Blocks

Draw a diagonal line across the wrong side of the following squares:

▸ (4) 3⅞" large yellow floral print squares

▸ (64) 3½" rose-pink tone-on-tone squares

▸ (32) 3½" light green print squares

Half-Square Triangle Four-Patch Blocks – Make Four

1. Place the light blue 3⅞" squares right sides together on the large yellow floral print 3⅞" squares. Sew a ¼" seam on each side of the drawn line. Cut on the drawn line. Open and press.

  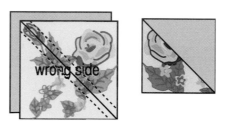

2. Refer to the drawing of the half-square triangle Four-Patch square. Sew a 3½" small yellow floral print square to the blue side of each half-square triangle square. Press. This will create one unit of the half-square triangle square.

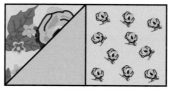

3. Place two of the sewn units right sides together with a 3½" square right sides together on the half-square triangle square. Sew together. Make four blocks and lay to the side.

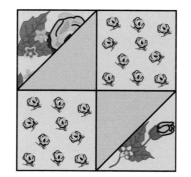

Center and Border Star Point Blocks – Make 16

1. Place the rose-pink 3½" squares with the drawn lines right sides together on the top right-hand side of the (16) 6½" small yellow floral print squares. Sew on the drawn line. Trim off the corner fabrics allowing a ¼" seam allowance. Open and press.

2. Repeat this process on the top left-hand side on each of the 16 squares. Lay to the side.

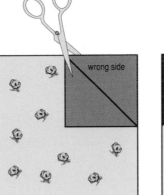
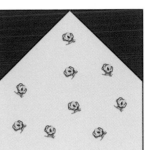

Four-Patch Star Point Squares – Make Eight

1. Sew the 2½" x 22" small yellow floral print strips to the 2½" x 22" small dark green print strips. Press.

2. Crosscut these sewn strips into (16) 2½" sections.

3. Pair the sections together with the small dark green print right sides together on the small yellow floral print square. Sew the two units together. Continue until eight Four-Patches are sewn. Open and press.

4. Cut each 7¼" rose-pink square twice on the diagonal for a total of 32 triangles.

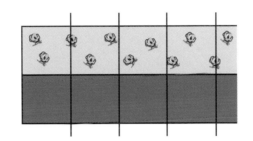

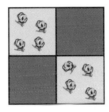

5. Center one of these rose-pink triangles, right sides together, on one side of the four-patch unit. Sew in place. Open and press.

6. Continue to sew triangles to each side of the Four-Patch unit until all sides are sewn and pressed. Make eight blocks.

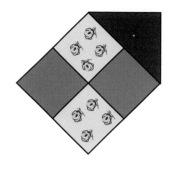
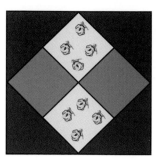

Star Center Units – Make Eight

Place a light green 3½" square with a drawn line right sides together on the top right-hand corner of a 6½" rose-pink square. Sew on the drawn line.

Trim off the back fabrics, leaving a ¼" seam allowance. Open and press. Repeat this process on all corners of the square

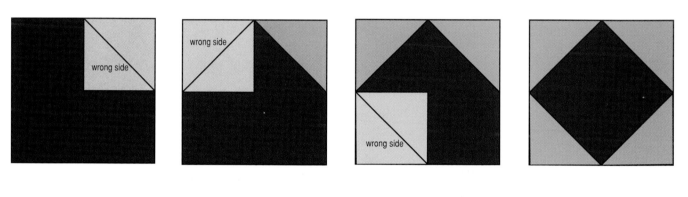

Building the Table Topper

1. Refer to the Bed of Roses Table Topper photo often.

2. Lay out each row of blocks as shown. There are seven rows of seven blocks.

3. Sew the blocks together into rows. Press.

4. Sew the rows together. Press.

Finishing the Table Topper

1. Layer and quilt the topper as desired. The model was quilted using a free-form quilted rose in the large yellow floral blocks; a medium meander stitch was used in the light areas of the quilt.

2. Sew the 2½" rose-pink tone-on-tone binding strips end-to-end.

3. Fold the binding wrong sides together and press.

4. Sew the raw edge of the binding to the outer edge of the table topper.

5. Fold the folded edge of the binding to the back of the quilt and hand or machine sew in place.

Green Gingham
Round Table Cover

68" Round Table Cover

This matching table cover is easily made by sewing two half-circle shapes together. The table cover matches the table top quilt beautifully.

Preparation

1. Read all instructions before you begin.
2. Wash and press all fabrics.
3. Use ¼" seams throughout.
4. Cutting instructions are based on 42" wide fabrics.

Fabric and Tools Needed

- 4⅔ yd. green check fabric
- Pencil and string
- Tissue paper and tape
- Basic sewing supplies, rotary cutter, cutting mat, and see-through ruler

Cutting and Assembly Instructions

1. Cut a 24" x 42" fabric piece from the 4⅔ yards of green check fabric to make bias strips.

2. Cut the remaining fabric into two 72" x 42" lengths. Place the fabric pieces right sides together. Sew the 72" length seam together. Fold in quarters.

3. Tape the tissue paper together to make a 40" square.

4. Tie a 38" length of string to the pencil and draw a quarter circle.

5. Cut out the paper pattern.

6. Pin the pattern on the folds of the fabric. Cut out the circle.

7. Cut enough 2" wide bias strips to measure 184 inches. Sew the bias strips end-to-end. Fold the bias binding strip, wrong sides together, lengthwise. Press.

8. Sew the raw edge of the binding to the wrong-side edge of the table cover.

9. Fold the binding to the right side and topstitch in place to finish.

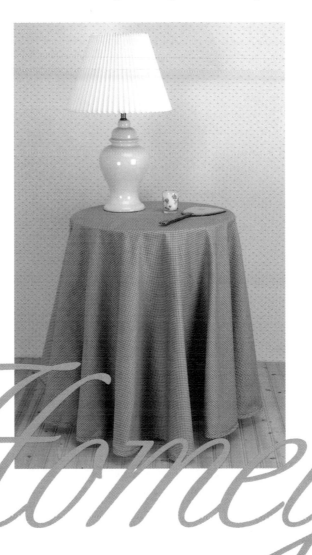

Sweet Dreams Picture

An 11" x 14" Vintage-Style Stitched Picture

Memories of loved ones abound whenever a hand-embroidered item is placed in view. This charming picture is easily stitched with embroidery floss colors that match the basic colors of the entire bedroom collection. Take some time out, sit awhile, and stitch this sweet sentiment to hang on the wall. Consider adding round wood ball feet to the back of the frame to make a delightful breakfast tray.

Preparation

1. Read all instructions before you begin.
2. Wash and press all fabrics.
3. Use ¼" seams throughout.
4. Press all seams in the direction that allows the seam to "lock" before continuing to build each portion of each block. Press all seams to the dark fabric when possible.
5. Cutting instructions are based on 42" wide fabrics.

Fabrics and Tools Needed

- Fat eighth Osnaburg for stitched background
- Fat eighths or scrap fabrics of small green, yellow, blue, and rose-pink prints for pieced border
- Fat quarter muslin for backing fabric
- 14" x 18" thin cotton batting
- 11" x 14" frame
- Embroidery floss in the following colors: rose-pink, medium sage green, dark green, blue, and gold
- Embroidery needle
- 6" to 8" embroidery hoop
- Plain paper and pencil
- Basic sewing supplies, rotary cutter, cutting mat, and see-through ruler

Cutting Instructions

From the yellow print, cut

- (2) 1¼" x 9½" strips for the first border
- (2) 1¼" x 8" strips for the first border

From the rose-pink and blue prints, cut

- (7) 2" squares for the pieced border

From the green print, cut

- (2) 2" x 11" strips for the outer side borders

Center Panel Instructions

1. Lay the plain piece of paper over the embroidery pattern and trace the pattern onto the paper.
2. Lay the Osnaburg fabric on the top of the traced pattern and trace the pattern onto the Osnaburg using the pencil.
3. Refer to the color photo of the stitched picture often.
4. Thread the embroidery needle with two strands of floss.
5. Stitch the design in place using the color and stitch stated. Refer to the stitch chart (page 19) for instructions on the individual stitches.

   ‣ Letters: Backstitch using sage green floss.
   ‣ Flowers: Lazy daisy stitch using rose-pink floss.
   ‣ Flower centers: Tie French knots using dark rose floss.
   ‣ Stems: Backstitch using dark green floss.
   ‣ Bird: Backstitch using blue floss.
   ‣ Bird beak: Backstitch using gold floss.
   ‣ Bird eye: Backstitch using black floss.

6. Cut the center panel to measure 6½" x 9½".

Old-fashioned

Building the Picture

First Border

Sew the 1¼" yellow print borders to the sides, top, and bottom of the stitched center panel. Press.

Pieced Border

Lay out the 2" rose-pink and blue print squares as shown on the color photo. Sew together and press. Sew the pieced borders to the top and bottom of the stitched center panel.

Side Borders

Sew the 2" x 11" green print side borders to the sides of the stitched center panel.

Finishing the Stitched Picture

1. Layer the batting between the top and muslin backing fabric.

2. Stipple quilt around the letters and other embroidered designs using a small stipple pattern. Continue to stipple the border areas using a larger stipple pattern.

3. Trim all backing and batting even with the top edges.

4. Remove the backing from the frame. Lay the quilted piece face down on the glass. Be sure to verify the top and bottom on the frame. Replace the cardboard and paper backing on the center of the frame. Bend the connectors to hold all layers securely.

Flower Basket
Fat Quarter Pillow

10½" x 18" Decorative Pillow

This long and narrow accent pillow is made by using a fat quarter as the base on which all of the appliqués are ironed. Decorative stitches are used to set off each shape and to add homey appeal.

Preparation

1. Read all instructions before you begin.
2. Wash and press all fabrics.
3. Use ¼" seams throughout.
4. Press seam allowances in the direction that allows the seam to "lock" before continuing to build each portion of each block. Press all seams to the dark fabric when possible.
5. Cutting instructions are based on 42" wide fabrics.

Fabrics and Tools Needed

- Fat quarter or 18" x 22" small green check for pillow
- Fat eighth tan plaid for basket appliqué
- Fat eighths or scrap fabrics of the following:
  - rose-pink print for flower and flower center appliqués
  - yellow print for flower and flower center appliqués
  - small dark green print for leaves and flower appliqués
- ½ yd. iron-on fusible web
- Embroidery floss: green and rose-pink
- Embroidery needle
- Polyester fiberfill stuffing
- Doily or lace (optional)
- Basic sewing supplies, rotary cutter, cutting mat, and see-through ruler

Cutting and Sewing Instructions

1. Trace three large flowers, three flower centers, five leaves, three stems, one basket, and one basket handle onto the iron-on fusible web. Trace the various appliqué shapes that require the same fabrics together on the fusible web.

2. Cut around each group of appliqués, allowing a ¼" excess.

3. Peel off the paper backing on the iron-on fusible web and iron the web to the wrong side of the fabrics selected for the appliqués.

4. Cut out each appliqué and remove the paper backing.

5. Fold the small green check fat quarter in half to measure 11" x 18". Fold again and press to find the center.

6. Arrange the appliqués on the green check background, center as desired, and iron in place.

7. Thread the embroidery needle with two strands of embroidery floss.

8. Stitch large blanket stitches around each appliqué using the green and rose-pink floss as shown in the photo.

9. Fold the 18" sides under ¼" and sew a hem. Overlap the hemmed edges and sew together leaving a 5" opening at the center.

10. Fold the center seam down the back of the pillow. Sew the top and bottom seams.

11. Stuff the pillow firmly with the polyester fiberfill. Hand sew the back opening shut

12. Hand stitch a small piece of doily or cotton lace to the basket if desired.

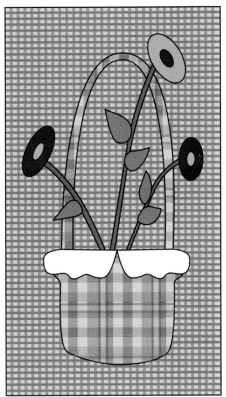

Decorative

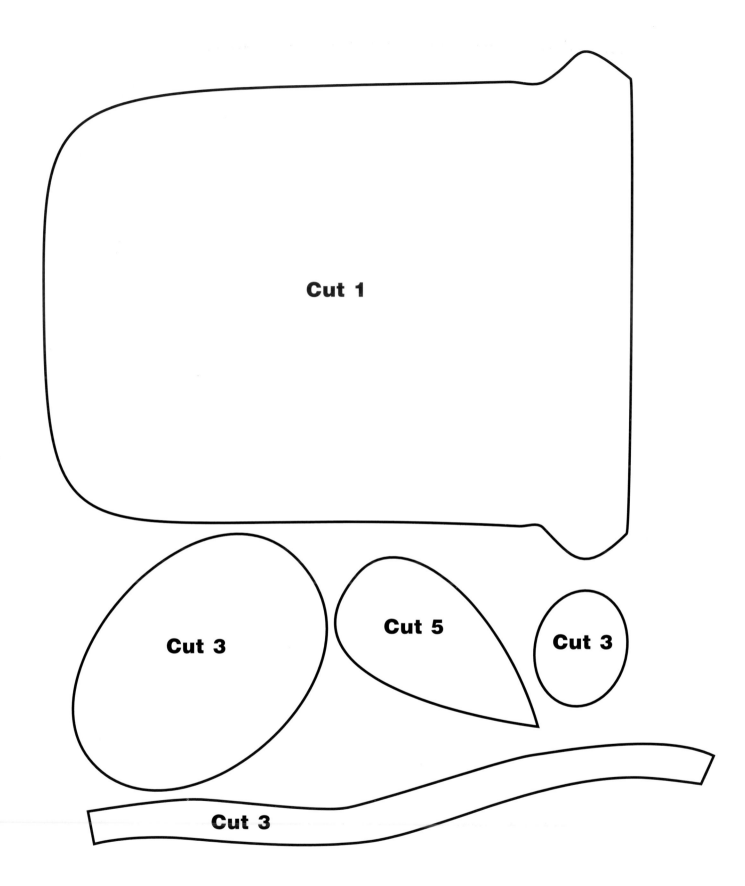

Cut 1

Cut 3

Cut 5

Cut 3

Cut 3

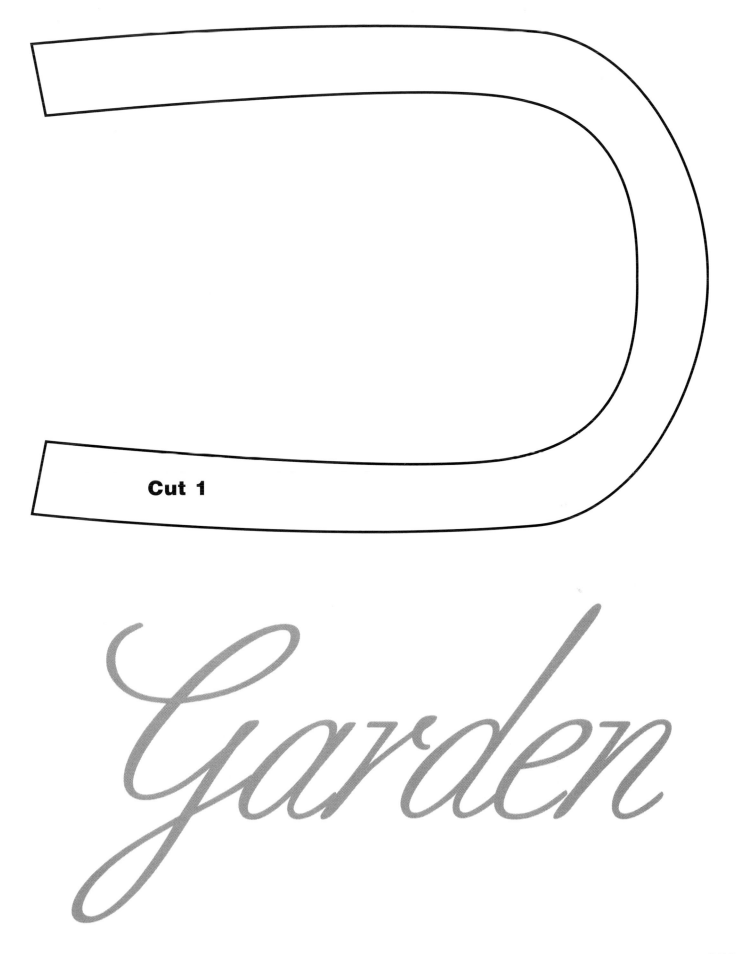

Cut 1

Garden

Garden Square Pillow

16" Square Accent Pillow

The masculine plaids of homespun fabric make the flower
center pop on this easy-to-assemble pillow. Add rows of fringe
as the final touch on this decorative pillow.

Preparation

1. Read all instructions before you begin.
2. Wash and press all fabrics.
3. Use ¼" seams throughout.
4. Press seam allowances in the direction that allows the seams to "lock" before continuing to build each portion of each block. Press all seams to the dark fabric when possible.
5. Cutting instructions are based on 42" wide fabrics.

Fabric and Tools Needed

- Fat eighth or 5" square blue print fabric for center square
- ⅛ yd. or 1½" x 23" green print for center square border
- Fat quarter tan plaid print for second border
- ¼ yd. green check for third border
- Fat quarter blue print for pillow back
- 16" pillow form and/or stuffing
- ¾ yd. decorative fringe (if desired)
- Basic sewing supplies, rotary cutter, cutting mat, and see-through ruler

Cutting Instructions

From the fat eighth blue print, cut

- (1) 5" square

From the green print, cut

- (1) 1½" x 23" strip

  From this strip, cut two 1½" x 5" sections and two 1½" x 6½" sections.

From the tan plaid fat quarter, cut

- (2) 3½" x 22" strips

  From these strips, cut two 3½" x 12½" strips and two 3½" x 6½" strips.

From the green check, cut

- (2) 2½" x 42" strips

  From these strips, cut two 2½" x 16½" strips and two 2½" x 12½" strips.

From the blue print fat quarter, cut

- (2) 9" x 16½" rectangles

Building the Pillow Top

1. Sew the 1½" x 5" green print strips to the right-hand and left-hand side of the 5" blue print square.
2. Sew the 1½" x 6½" green print strips to the top and bottom of the 5" blue print square.
3. Sew the 3½" x 6½" tan plaid border strips to the top and bottom of the center square.
4. Sew the 3½" x 12½" tan plaid border strips to the sides of the center square.
5. Sew the 2½" x 12½" green check third border strips to the sides of the center square.

6. Sew the 2½" x 16½" green check third border strips to the top and bottom to finish the pillow top.
7. Sew the fringe to the sides of the tan plaid border.

Building the Pillow Back

1. Fold one of the edges on the 16" side of the 9" x 16" rectangle under ¼" and sew a hem. Repeat with the remaining 9" x 16" rectangle.
2. Place the two hemmed edges on top of each other and sew the two together on each end about 3½".

Finishing the Pillow

1. Place the pillow back and the pillow front right sides together. Sew together around the entire pillow.
2. Turn right side out.
3. Insert the pillow form into the pillow through the back opening.
4. Hand sew the opening shut.

Yo-Yo Posy Pillow

9" Accent Pillow

Stitch up some yo-yos and create a touch of nostalgia in another accent pillow. Making yo-yos is an easy project that can travel with you anywhere. The dimension of the pillow is another fun design element in this project.

Preparation

1. Read all instructions before you begin.
2. Wash and press all fabrics.
3. Use ¼" seams throughout.

Fabric and Tools Needed

- ⅓ yd. blue floral print
- ⅛ yd. or scraps green and yellow
- ¼ yd. rose-pink print
- 12" doily
- Polyester fiberfill stuffing
- 9" paper plate
- Paper to trace yo-yo pattern

Cutting Instructions

1. Trace around the 9" paper plate to make the top and back of the pillow.
2. Trace the yo-yo pattern (page 124) onto a plain piece of paper. Cut out the paper yo-yo for the pattern.
3. Cut three yellow print yo-yos.
4. Cut 15 rose-pink yo-yos.
5. Cut 12 green check yo-yos.

Sewing Instructions

1. Place the two 9" fabric circles right sides together. Sew around leaving a 4" opening for turning and stuffing. Turn right sides out. Stuff the pillow tightly. Hand sew the opening shut.
2. Place the 12" doily on the pillow top. Hand tack the doily in place.
3. Double thread the needle with two strands of thread that match the yo-yo.
4. Place the right side of the yo-yo down. Fold the outer edge of the yo-yo inside about ⅛". Hand sew large gathering stitches around the outer edge of the yo-yo. Pull the gathering stitches tightly. Tie off and cut the threads short. Continue until all of the cut yo-yos are gathered. (See page 20 for more information on making yo-yos.)
5. Refer to the photo for layout. Pin the yo-yos in place on the pillow top as shown.
6. Hand sew each yo-yo in place by stitching small tack stitches to connect and hold the yo-yo to the pillow top.

Nostalgia

Yo-Yo
Pattern

Create

About the Author

Pearl Louise Krush grew up in Whitewood, South Dakota. She was very active in 4-H and was surrounded by family members who encouraged her in the craft and hobby industry where she was the designer and project manager for two lace companies for several years. She started Pearl Louise Designs pattern company in the late-1980s. She continues to run the pattern company, free-lance design for magazine and book publishers, and develop kits and gift designs. She also owns the Thimble Cottage Quilt Shop in Rapid City, South Dakota. She enjoys fishing with her husband, Fred, whenever time allows.

Pearl loves to teach and had a great time teaching on a segment of Quilt Central, an educational television program with Cindy Walter. Pearl's appearances can be seen on PBS stations nationwide.

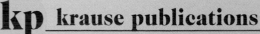